fresh from Vermont

Fresh from Vermont

VERMONT LIFE MAGAZINE'S
SEASONAL COOKBOOK

RECIPES FROM
NEW ENGLAND CULINARY INSTITUTE
AND CHEF DAVID MILES

TEXT BY
MARIALISA CALTA

Inquiries should be addressed to
Vermont Life, 6 Baldwin Street, Montpelier, VT 05602.
Printed in the United States of America.
First edition.
1 2 3 4 5 6 7 8 9 10

Design and art direction by The Laughing Bear Associates, Montpelier, Vermont
Photography by Becky Luigart-Stayner, Burlington, Vermont
Formatting and index by Electric Dragon Productions, Montpelier, Vermont

Library of Congress Cataloging-in-Publication Data
Fresh from Vermont: recipes / by the New England Culinary Institute;
introduction by Marialisa Calta.
p.   cm.
Includes index.
ISBN 0-936896-24-8
1. Cookery, American — New England style. 2. Cookery — Vermont.
I. New England Culinary Institute.
TX15.2.N48F74   1992
641.5974—dc20   92-33516
CIP

CONTENTS

INTRODUCTION

What do Vermonters eat? That depends on just which typical Vermonter you have in mind. The Archetypal Vermonter, that flannel-shirted fellow with the cow manure on his work boots, eats pots of baked beans laced with maple syrup and dishes of salt pork with milk gravy. The Sixties Vermonter, that young woman/man in Birkenstocks and natural fibers tending her/his organic garden, survives on granola, tofu, and sprouts. The Backwoods Vermonter, the one with the gun rack in his pickup and the deer slung over the fender, chows down on venison and beer. The Yuppie Vermonter? Sea urchins with papaya glaze and a glass of designer water, thank you.

But what do *real* Vermonters — the actual people who live and work and hunt and fish and garden and raise families here — what do *they* eat? They eat all and none of the above and more: fish sticks and fresh salmon, Cheese Doodles and aged cheddar, McDonald's and maple mousse. Vermonters eat, in short, just about like people in the rest of the country. But what distinguishes Vermont cookery is a culinary tradition that stresses economy, ingenuity, adaptability, and an open mind. It's a tradition with a long history. Before the advent of refrigeration and preservatives, foods were generally enjoyed on a seasonal basis: when the rhubarb came in, Vermonters ate rhubarb. There was no running down to the market for a pound of kiwi or star fruit.

THE DISTINCTIVE STYLE OF VERMONT COOKERY IS LIKE THE STATE ITSELF — SEASONAL, INFORMAL, BASED ON LONG-HELD RURAL TRADITIONS AND A DEVOTION TO THE HIGHEST QUALITY. IT'S A COMBINATION THAT CAN MAKE A SIMPLE MEAL SEEM SPECIAL.

Of course, fruits and vegetables were put by for the winter; Beatrice Vaughan, a Vermont cook and author of *Yankee Hill Country Cooking*, wrote that "it was considered a poor year if less than four or five hundred quarts of vegetables and fruit were not put away down cellar." But freshness was prized, and Vermonters gorged on fresh produce and fresh meat when they could.

The long, cold winters here enabled families to freeze much of their food; Vaughan described her great-grandmother brewing soup in a kettle and setting it in the frigid back pantry. "In the center of the kettle she stood upright a wooden paddle having a hole in the end of its handle," Vaughan wrote. "When the soup had frozen to granite hardness, great-grandmother warmed the outside of the kettle just enough to slide the icy lump out intact. The frozen mass was hung by slipping the hole in the handle over a nail in a high beam. When soup was needed, she merely chopped off a hunk with the hatchet and heated it with the requisite amount of water." Meat could be kept frozen through most of the winter, and the rest of the year cooks used ham, bacon, the ubiquitous salt pork, and other cured meats and salted fish in the most inventive manner possible.

It is best, however, not to romanticize the meals of yore, a point well made by Louise Andrews Kent, an "adopted Vermonter," to use her own phrase, and a resident of Kents Corner, a settlement in the town of Calais. Kent, a prodigious writer who wrote cookbooks under the name of Mrs. Appleyard of the fictional community "Appleyard Center," wrote in *The Vermont Year Round Cookbook* (1965) of the old-time general store, with its dinner staples of salt fish, salt pork, pickles, Montpelier crackers, and potatoes.

The stores, she wrote, were "dark, dingy, untidy and smelling of kerosene," a flavor that often pervaded the merchandise. The kerosene can had a potato on the end of its spout. "This was to keep the kerosene from spilling. It served its purpose, but when the storekeeper had to fill a lard pail one of the customers had brought, he had to re-move the potato. "Where did he put it? In the handiest place, natu-rally — on top of the cracker barrel or the flour barrel or the sugar bin or on a firkin of butter — or, most natural of all — in the potato bin.

"There was a Vermont conversation a half century ago that went like this: 'When did you have your potatoes?' 'We had them at night' or 'we had them at noon. Potatoes, in fact, with codfish or salt pork, were your *pièce de résistance,* and they were often subtly flavored with kerosene." So much for romance.

And yet historian Charles Morrissey has written that "Vermont is an experience to live as well as a state to live in," and there is truth to that. Bernard DeVoto called Vermont a special world, and indeed it is to the half million or so people who have been lucky enough to have been born here and/or smart enough to choose it as a place to live. There is more than a grain of truth to the notion that life in this rolling, rugged place has produced a certain kind of character in its people, and that there is a kind of hardscrabble nobility to be found here. "Country life does not always have breadth, but it has depth," wrote Calvin Coolidge (born and raised in Plymouth Notch, Vermont) in his autobiography. "It is neither artificial nor superficial, but is kept close to the realities."

And it is hard to imagine anyone but a Vermonter, in this case former governor and U.S. Senator George D. Aiken, saying, "But, after all, problems are what make life worth living." "Yankee ingenuity" and "Yankee thrift" are more than just clichés. They exist, and there are people schooled in these old-fashioned virtues who are running not only dairy farms but computer companies, retail stores, restaurants, and craft cooperatives.

Many entrepreneurs have chosen food as their business. The number of speciality food producers in the state has grown astonishingly from about 15 in 1984, the year the state started keeping records, to more than 200. In the last decade, the number of restaurants has grown by more than 200 to nearly 2000.

With its roots in agriculture, Vermont has always been a state where good food was available. Dairy farms, now in decline, provided Vermonters with fresh milk, cream, butter, and cheese. Family farms produced their own meat, poultry, vegetables, and eggs. Even today, Vermont leads the nation in maple syrup production. Apple orchards still abound, providing eating apples and fodder for the state's cider mills. Vermont beekeepers lead New England in the production of honey. Cheesemakers have branched out from traditional Vermont cheddar into low-fat cheeses, goat cheese, marscarpone, and fromage blanc. Lamb, pork, veal, fallow deer, fish, and game birds are locally farmed. Berries ripen in abundance and pick-your-own operations thrive in the summer. Hunters stock their own larders, and those of their friends and neighbors, with venison, wild turkey, and bear. Fishermen in search of freshwater fish ply the waters of Lake Champlain and the multitude of streams and rivers that crisscross the state.

Aside from new restaurants and food producers, Vermont has a proud culinary tradition embodied in church dinners and community suppers. The cuisine at many community events reflects the state's rich cultural heritage: from the French, who brought pea soup and meat pies; to the Italians, who introduced mostaccioli and polenta; and the Scots and Welsh, who brought scones and oatmeal bread. And, of course, sugaring—the making of maple syrup and a showcase of the Yankee work ethic—was first practiced by Native Americans.

Nowadays, ethnic influences are seeping across Vermont's borders in smaller numbers, with out-of-staters moving in, each with his or her own heritage—Asian, Greek, Latino, Slavic, African American, Indian—and a taste for exotic cuisine cultivated in the country's metropolitan areas. The state's specialty food producers include not just the traditional sugarmakers but now producers of salsa, European-style chocolates, vinaigrettes, and flavored mustards.

It was Lucy Emerson of Montpelier who put Vermont on the nation's culinary map in 1808 by writing what food historians consider America's first regional cookbook. It's a tiny volume, now in a vault at the Vermont Historical Society, entitled *The New-England Cookery, or The Art of Dressing All Kinds of Flesh, Fish and Vegetables and the Best Modes of Making Pastes, Puffs, Pies, Tarts, Puddings, Custards and Preserves and All Kinds of Cakes From the Imperial Plum to Plain Cake.*

According to writers John and Karen Hess, Ms. Emerson apparently lifted most of her recipes from a 1796 volume, *American Cookery*, by Amelia Simmons of Hartford, Connecticut. But she set the stage for countless Vermonters—most of them women—who contributed recipes to church and community cookbooks that still overflow shelves in many a Vermont kitchen. Their books make for interesting reading not only for the recipes—for fishballs, raspberry shrub, salsify fritters, and cabbage stew—but for the cooking hints ("a spoonful of stewed tomatoes in the gravy of either roasted or fried meats is an improvement"), housekeeping advice, and advertisements.

The Green Mountain Cookbook, compiled by The Ladies of the Congregational Church of Fair Haven in 1902, contains an ad for Dr. Jones' Beaver Oil, touted as a cure for "rheumatism, neuralgia, toothache, swellings, lumbago, corns and bunions, colic and cramps, burns and scalds, wounds and sprains, dreadful bruises, quinzy and sore throat, sick and nervous headache, colds in chest and lungs, crick in back, lameness and weakness, etc." One wonders not only how one used this miracle oil, but what "etc." could possibly include.

But it is Mrs. Appleyard, blessed with a quick wit and a keen eye for the Vermont landscape, who provides some of the most interesting reading along with many recipes that have stood the test of time. She wove them into prose remarkable for its sense of place. Vermont's beauty, she once wrote, "is in the bones of the land, in its enduring and compelling power." In *Mrs. Appleyard's Winter Kitchen,* for example, she described an October snowstorm:

> Elms were great golden wine glasses, maples had turned into rainbows without a leaf lost, birches and poplars were still delicately green just spangled with gold. Beeches were orange and bronze. Over them one night snow sifted quietly down. The next morning the hills were not a sight easily forgotten. The snow was not deep. On hayfields and lawns the grass underneath gave it a strange greenish tone as if northern lights were flickering over it.

Fresh from Vermont attempts to convey some of the sense of Vermont in its seasonal glories in words that, it is hoped, will ring true to those who live here, will reawaken memories in those who have visited, and inspire interest in those who have not.

Chef David Miles of the New England Culinary Institute in Montpelier has created recipes to reflect the variety of Vermont's culinary heritage and the range of its expanding gastronomic frontiers. He has offered updated versions of such traditional delights as red flannel hash and baked beans, and more contemporary dishes like linguine primavera with morels and fiddleheads. Though up-to-date in their style and execution, these recipes stress the old-fashioned notion of taking advantage of seasonal bounty. They are examples, in their breadth and variety, of what Vermonters eat.

New England Culinary Institute

꙳

Fifteen years ago, just about the only place to get a cup of coffee in Montpelier after 9 o'clock on a Sunday night was from the vending machine at Bob's Sunoco. Then, in 1980, the New England Culinary Institute burst on the scene. Coffee, ha! How about a cup of espresso? Capuccino, perhaps? Café au lait? It was clear that, culinarily speaking, things in Montpelier were looking up.

At the center of this culinary revolution were two men, Francis Voigt and John Dranow, refugees from the cutbacks at Goddard College in Plainfield, where Voigt had been an administrator, Dranow, a teacher. They combined talents to search for a business to run. They looked at the possibility of breweries; Dranow says now he spent a good deal of time back then brewing "really terrible beer." They considered deer farming, even running an auto body shop. Then, as Dranow tells it, the Central Vermont Economic Development Agency planted the idea of a cooking school.

CHEF DAVID MILES IN THE KITCHEN OF THE NEW ENGLAND CULINARY INSTITUTE IN MONTPELIER. SINCE ITS FOUNDING IN 1980, THE INSTITUTE HAS ESTABLISHED ITSELF AS ONE OF THE NATION'S LEADING COOKING SCHOOLS.

"We liked the idea," says Dranow. "We both came from education and we both loved food." Research showed there were jobs for qualified chefs going begging. "It was like going through the looking glass," says Dranow. "I went to graduate school when there were five or six Ph.D.s per job; and I found that in the world of chefs it was reversed."

He began making phone calls to people in the food industry. "The response was unbelievable," says Dranow. "People told us that if we could produce a graduate with good practical skills, discipline, and a willingness to work hard, they'd welcome us with open arms." Dranow and Voigt, with the support of their wives, poets Ellen Bryant Voigt and Louise Gluck, decided to go ahead. They took out second mortgages on their homes and used what Dranow describes as their minimal life savings to rent an office over a Montpelier tavern and begin hiring staff. Their wives supported them through teaching jobs at various universities around the country.

The program that Voigt and Dranow developed, with the help of their first employee, program director Howard Fisher, followed Voigt's vision of incorporating two educational models: the European apprenticeship and the university hospital.

"My father was a doctor and he always talked about the vocational approach to medical education," says Voigt. "At NECI we wanted the classes to supplement the hands-on training, not the reverse." The school prides itself on what Voigt believes is the lowest student-teacher ratio of any culinary school in the country (7 to 1), and on a hands-on approach to cooking that leaves graduates well prepared for life in a professional kitchen. A required internship program — students spend two 6-month stints during the 2-year course working at restaurants — helps complete the educational experience, as does time logged as chefs, waiters, and sommeliers in the school's own working restaurants. Classes in such culinary subjects as cooking theory, baking, pastry, and garde manger are supplemented by courses in the history of food and wine, basic math, and an English course that teaches writing and such skills as word processing and résumé writing.

The school also prides itself on being the only cooking school in the country with a physical education requirement, a 24-week "Health and Wellness Independent Study" that is devised by each student and approved by the faculty. This was instituted to promote fitness and health and to combat the historical stereotype of the stout, heavy-drinking chef. Students who complete the two-year program, or who successfully finish an advanced placement curriculum, are awarded an Associate's Degree of Occupational Studies in Culinary Arts.

The school—which in the beginning consisted of Dranow, Voigt, Fisher, and Michel LeBorgne, a French-trained chef who was the first instructor and is now vice president for culinary affairs—opened in June 1980 with six students, who lived with LeBorgne at a Montpelier hotel and took their classes in the hotel kitchen. By 1982, the school had reached its maximum capacity of 30 students per class or 120 students. By 1983, it moved to its current location, in a former alternative high school on a hill overlooking Montpelier, and enlarged its capacity to about 200. (The school has approximately 100 students, half first year and half second year, on campus at any time.)

Attention was being paid: Julia Child spoke at graduation, and in 1985, NECI was asked to create a cake for President Reagan's second inauguration, a 6-×-8-×-3–foot extravanganza in the shape of the U.S. Capitol. "It served 20,000 people," says Dranow. "I know because I served every piece myself." Phase I of NECI's growth plan had been completed. The school had made a name for itself.

Voigt did not want to enlarge the school because he thought such a move would diminish the small-school feeling. Maintaining a hands-on program and a low student-teacher ratio was paramount. So the administrators devised a plan to more or less clone NECI, giving birth to a second campus at The Inn at Essex in the Burlington suburb of Essex. In September 1989 the facility opened with a nearly identical curriculum and an identical student-teacher ratio of 7 to 1. By 1991, the Essex campus had reached its capacity of 200 students. In this way, Voigt explains, the school was able to increase its income from tuition without incurring additional administrative expenses. Salaries, he says, are now competitive with other top cooking schools.

Between the two campuses, the school runs several restaurants and food-service establishments and catering services in both Montpelier and Essex. In addition, students at the Essex campus gain supplemental experience in buffet and banquet work.

Now that the second campus is up and running, Dranow and Voigt are thinking about future improvements. They talk about the possibility of seminars for food writers, plans to expand the school's roster of classes for the community, and of continuing education courses for working chefs.

Voigt, however, is ever vigilant against the notion of "growth for the sake of growth." Dranow says each step along the way for this relatively young institution has had its share of difficulties. "And it will continue to be hard if we continue striving," he says. "We can't be the biggest, or the richest, or the oldest. But we *can* be the best."

Chef David Miles

John Dranow, cofounder and chief operating officer at the New England Culinary Institute, describes the new breed of American chefs as "creative, educated, thoughtful, and interested in the world." By this definition, David Miles, who created the recipes for this book, is one of the new breed.

Born in 1954 and raised in New York City and Rockland County, New York, Miles says he was drawn to cooking at a young age. "My parents encouraged me," he says. "They traveled a lot and were exposed to a wide variety of foods. And they encouraged their children to find out for themselves what they wanted to do." Nonetheless, Miles did not set out to pursue a career in the field until he graduated from Goddard College, in Plainfield, Vermont, and went back to New York. There he began working in restaurants and studying culinary arts at New York City Community College.

"It's a satisfying craft," says Miles. "You see improvement, and results. You get immediate reaction and feedback to your work."

In 1982, he says, he and Deborah Dwyer, his wife and fellow Goddard graduate, decided they had had enough of the city and wanted to return to Vermont. "I had heard good things about the school," says Miles of his decision to answer an ad for a chef/instructor at the New England Culinary Institute. Arriving in Montpelier, he started as a chef/instructor at Tubbs restaurant, owned by the school. He then developed the school's course in cooking theory, teaching what he calls "the hows and whys" of cooking. But he wanted to be back in the kitchen, so he returned to another Institute restaurant, Elm Street Café, where he contributed for almost 4 years. Now he teaches a course in meat fabrication, which includes the butchering of meat and fish, curing, smoking, and sausage making.

Miles, tall and lean, tends toward the serious, a demeanor alleviated by a wide and frequent grin. Watching him with students, one sees a teacher who is intense, interested, informal yet demanding. He finds being responsible for the education of young chefs more challenging than simply working in a restaurant kitchen. "In a restaurant kitchen, you're constantly teaching, anyway," he says. "But here, I am more aware of my responsibilities. It would be hard not to take that seriously." When he is not in the classroom he is home with his wife and two young daughters. One might also find him, depending on the time of year, on a trout stream, basketball court, or softball diamond, or walking in the woods in search of wild mushrooms.

Presented with the idea for this book, Miles says he set out to "represent the quality foods available in Vermont and people's historical interest in food in the state." The recipes were developed to make them "accessible to people, not overly complicated or daunting."

Despite the recent recognition of some chefs as celebrities, and an increased awareness among many consumers of exotic cuisines and new food trends, Miles says that "in the old days, people took food seriously, too."

"There have been good home cooks in New England for hundreds of years," he adds. He developed recipes to reflect that tradition and to rely heavily on the precept that "you use what you have in season." "It's just plain good sense," he says, "and the result is good food."

SUMMER

It is fitting that Independence Day occurs in July because summer is Vermont's season of freedom: freedom from winter clothes, the tyranny of the furnace and wood stove, freedom from mud and snow and ice, from flu outbreaks, dead batteries, and frozen pipes. Of course, there is a price to pay for such freedom. It is extracted in late May or early June by the black fly, that bloodthirsty insect that does not so much bite as carve into the exposed skin of children at play and gardeners at work. Next comes a visit from the black fly's comrade-in-arms, the mosquito. Then, there is the tyranny of the garden itself, with its required tilling, mulching, planting, thinning, weeding, and, if you're lucky, harvesting.

But there is more freedom: the incomparable, exhilarating freedom, when faced on a warm summer evening with the bounty of a garden in full production, of choosing a menu for a meal that will, by virtue of its freshness and flavor, inspire dreams in midwinter. The Vermont landscape, distinct in each season, is transformed in summer into a monotonously rich expanse of green. I have read that landscape painters who come to Vermont complain about all the green they are required to use, but it seems to me that the subtle variations required for pine, maple, fern, moss, and grass would be a great challenge.

In Vermont, summer starts sometime at the end of January when the seed catalogs begin jamming mailboxes already crowded with overdue heating bills and credit card statements. A gardener can forget the bills while planting a dream garden of Early Girls and Better Boys, Kentucky Wonders, and De-

ENJOY VERMONT'S SHORT, BEAUTIFUL SUMMERS WITH AN ELEGANT PICNIC LIKE THIS ONE AT SHELBURNE FARMS. THIS SPACIOUS ESTATE ON LAKE CHAMPLAIN IS NOW THE SITE OF SUMMER CONCERTS, AN INN, AND A WORKING FARM.

troit Dark Reds. Summer has to start early; it's a short season here, and residents extend their pleasure by anticipating it months in advance. Seedlings are started indoors at Town Meeting Day, the first Tuesday in March. And there is nothing like a set of paper cups sprouting tomato plants to make a person feel summery.

Vermont gardens compensate for the short growing season by producing certain things in abundance: green beans, for example, peas, and the ubiquitous zucchini. In years past, gardeners canned their produce to last through the winter; now freezing is generally the method of choice. It is another aspect of the tyranny of the garden that on a hot, muggy night in August gardeners find themselves slaving over steaming kettles, blanching vegetables or making jam. The payoff comes in winter, though, when spreading summer-in-a-jar on toast or eating a still-crunchy (if you've done it right) platter of green beans.

Summer brings the smell of new-mown hay, the sweaty, scratchy work of haying, the excitement of racing with a thunderstorm to get the bales under cover. In the old days, haying had its own culinary imperative: the making of switchel, a kind of old-fashioned Gatorade containing cold water, cider vinegar, molasses, and ginger. A passage in the *Coolidge-Country Cookbook* describes it:

> During the hot summer days of haying women prepared and carried out in wooden jugs to the men working in the fields a drink known as switchel. . . . Cool, sweet and tart, it refreshed the hayers, and for a few brief moments both men and scythes sat motionless on the ground.

Yet another summer freedom is eating outdoors: a small bit of heaven for children and nirvana for parents tired of the indoor mess. Table manners are relaxed; just hose the little ones down after the meal! The dress code is relaxed, too; there is nothing like eating fresh corn in a just-dried bathing suit to make a diner feel at peace with the world. Menus need not be so carefully planned—a potpourri of fresh summer tastes, from potatoes to snap peas, corn, barbecued ribs, and tomato salad, would please all but the most quarrelsome palates.

It seems to me that summer truly belongs to children. I spent my childhood summers on the New Jersey shore, and the sights and sounds are indelibly imprinted in my mind: the boardwalk at Asbury Park replete with a panoply of smells (fried dough, cotton candy, seaweed), sounds (carousel music, ocean waves, salesmen hawking Vege-matics), and tastes (Italian ice, saltwater taffy, mussels in tomato sauce and garlic). I wonder what my children will remember of their Vermont summers. The way fireflies can, on certain magical evenings, make an entire field sparkle. The sound of fresh peas shelled into a metal pan? The sweet smell of new-mown hay? The way the grass in the field scratches their ankles and the whoosh of bats at the local pond, swooping down to check out late-night swimmers? The smell of the midway at a county fair (popcorn, cow manure, stale beer)?

Quite possibly they will remember their parents, hunched over the ground, an expanse of sunburned, bug-bitten flesh exposed, tending a patch of growth more like a small jungle than a garden; and then steaming the wallpaper off the kitchen walls in a frenzy of blanching and freezing. They will probably think we were crazy. But I hope they will remember how good summer tasted, those summers in Vermont.

Corn: A Summer Treat

The best way to get fresh corn is to grow it yourself. If you do, you can put the water on the stove, dash out to the garden, zip back to the kitchen, and husk the ears just as the water reaches a boil. The second best way to get fresh corn is to buy it from a farm stand. Any farm stand operator worth your business picks corn, not just once but several times a day, to ensure maximum freshness.

Bill Moynihan, at Ellie's Farm Stand in Northfield, picks corn at least three times a day, sometimes four and five times a day. "It's about the only thing I do some days — run back and forth for corn," he says. He explains: "As soon, and I mean *as soon* as it's picked, the sugar in that corn starts turning to starch, and the sugar is where the taste is."

He will sell no corn after its time. "People say it's just as good if you refrigerate it overnight," he says, pausing. "These tend to be, well, urban people, I guess. Being a farmer, it just won't do. Corn should be eaten fresh or not at all. You have to look at corn as a delicacy."

Andrew Nemethy, a writer and self-described "cornophile," who lives in Adamant, agrees. "With the possible exception of early peas, no other vegetable gives the burst of flavor and is as succulent as corn," says Nemethy. After a moment, he amends that statement: "Maybe asparagus, too. But asparagus wears on you. Corn doesn't."

An avid and expert gardener, Nemethy does not grow corn because it requires so much space and because "the raccoons always pick it the day before you were planning to." Instead, he has made a science of selecting the best ears from local farm stands. "It's completely unpredictable," he says. "One day you might have great corn, and three days later you get a lousy batch."

It's that "great" corn he lives for. "When I pick out a great batch, and I know I have a dozen ears to eat," says Nemethy, "well, then I'm a happy man."

Nemethy, like Karen Moynihan, advocates husking corn at the last minute and then plunging it in plain (no salt, no sugar, no milk) boiling water for 5 to 10 minutes. (Nemethy advocates 8.) "The biggest mistake people make with corn is overcooking it," says Moynihan. "Well, the *biggest* mistake is buying it in the grocery store because there is no hope for that stuff, no matter how you cook it."

The microwave also serves, and here are Moynihan's directions: wrap each husked ear in microwave-safe plastic wrap, keeping the ends of the wrap open, not closed up tight. Cook the corn on the high setting for 1 minute, then turn each ear over and cook it for 1½ minutes on the second side. Remove it from the plastic wrap immediately, or else it will keep cooking.

Eating corn is another matter. Nemethy prefers dotting an ear with unsalted butter, then adding a bit of salt, which, he says, "is different than using salted butter and no salt, or salted butter and a bit of salt." He never uses pepper. And he prefers the straight-across "typewriter" method as "most efficient" way to eat it. Nemethy has perfected his methods over many meals of corn, once eating 13 ears at one sitting. "I've never subscribed to the notion of corn as a side dish," he says. "To me it's the main event."

Spaghetti with Spinach (or Arugula), Tomatoes, and Romano

Use the arugula for a sharper taste. Serves 3 to 4.

½ cup olive oil
1 medium onion, diced
6 cloves garlic, minced
4 ripe tomatoes or 8 plum tomatoes, peeled, seeded, and diced
3 cups spinach or arugula or a mixture, chopped
freshly ground black pepper
1 pound spaghetti
1 cup grated Romano cheese

1

Bring 1 gallon salted water to a boil. Add spaghetti.

2

Meanwhile, in a large saucepan over medium heat, heat olive oil. Add onion and cook until clear. Add garlic and cook until fragrant. Add tomatoes and greens and cook until greens are wilted and still brightly colored. Season with salt and pepper.

3

When spaghetti is al dente, drain and add to tomato mixture. Toss well and heat gently, stirring for a few minutes. Remove from heat and add half the Romano.

4

Serve on warmed plates, season with a little more freshly ground black pepper and the remaining Romano. Serve with lightly toasted, buttered sourdough bread.

LINGUINE WITH LITTLENECK CLAMS

THE HOT CHILI SPICES UP AN ITALIAN FAVORITE. SERVES 3 TO 4.

---

2 to 3 dozen littleneck clams, shucked, juice strained, and reserved
or canned clams
¾ cup olive oil
1 medium onion, finely diced
⅓ cup garlic, minced
1 dried hot chili, seeds removed, and crushed into small pieces
2 teaspoons fresh thyme or 1 teaspoon dried thyme
½ cup white wine
½ cup Italian parsley, chopped
2 tablespoons unsalted butter
salt
freshly ground black pepper
1 pound linguine

1

In a 6-quart pot, bring salted water to a boil. Add linguine and cook until al dente.

2

Meanwhile, in a heavy skillet over medium heat, heat olive oil, onion, garlic, and chili flakes. When the smallest pieces of garlic turn amber, add ½ cup of reserved clam juice, thyme, and white wine. Simmer for 3 to 4 minutes.

3

Add clams and parsley and cook until clams are just heated through and parsley is bright. Whisk in butter and adjust the seasonings. Salt to taste.

4

Add drained linguine and toss well. Heat for 1 to 2 minutes. Serve in heated soup bowls and top with freshly ground black pepper.

NEW POTATO SALAD

A SUMMER CLASSIC. THE RADISHES ADD ZIP. SERVES 4, TWICE.

— ❧ —

3 pounds new potatoes
1 medium green pepper, cored, seeds and membrane removed, finely diced
3 scallions, white and 1 inch of green part, sliced
6 radishes, ends trimmed, quartered, cut into ⅛-inch slices
salt
freshly ground black pepper
2 ribs celery, peeled and finely diced
2 tablespoons Dijon mustard
½ cup mayonnaise
few drops lemon juice
¼ cup sour cream
chopped chives for garnish
hard-cooked eggs (optional)

1

Cover new potatoes with cold, salted water and bring to a simmer in a large pot. Cook gently until potatoes are tender. Drain, cool, and peel. Cut into ½-inch cubes. Combine with pepper, scallions, radish, and celery. Toss and season lightly with salt and pepper.

2

In a small mixing bowl, combine mustard and mayonnaise, whisk in lemon juice, and gently fold in sour cream. Add dressing to potatoes and mix well. Adjust seasoning, sprinkle with chives and chopped hard-cooked eggs, if desired. Cool before serving.

SCRAMBLED EGGS WITH SMOKED TROUT

THE SMOKY TROUT FLAVOR CARRIES THIS DISH
FAR BEYOND THE ORDINARY. SERVES 4.

❧

9 large eggs, room temperature
dash Tabasco
2 tablespoons unsalted butter
1 medium smoked trout, skinned, boned, and broken into flakes
3 tablespoons heavy cream or half and half
1 tablespoon chives, cut
freshly ground black pepper

1

In a small mixing bowl, beat together the eggs, water, and Tabasco with a fork.

2

In a nonstick skillet over medium high heat, add butter and cook until it foams. Add the eggs and cook, stirring, for 1 to 2 minutes. Lower the heat to medium and continue to cook until the eggs form small, soft curds. Add the trout and stir in to heat through. Add the heavy cream and mix well.

3

Portion eggs onto heated plates and garnish with chives and pepper. Serve with bagels and cream cheese or buttered toast and fresh fruit salad or melon.

GRILLED SWORDFISH, ROSEMARY, GOAT CHEESE, AND PEPPERS

THE MEATY SWORDFISH PROVIDES A PERFECT FOIL
FOR THE GOAT CHEESE. SERVES 4 TO 10.

---

four to ten 8-ounce, 1-inch-thick swordfish steaks
olive oil
salt
freshly ground black pepper
1 tablespoon fresh rosemary, chopped or ½ tablespoon dried rosemary
1 red pepper
1 yellow pepper
⅜ to ½ cup mild goat cheese, softened at room temperature
butter for basting
lemon wedges

1

Roast peppers under a broiler or over an open flame until the skin is blistered and charred uniformly. Place peppers in a paper bag and close the top. Let steam for 10 minutes to loosen the skin and then peel and remove the seeds and cut into thin strips. Cool.

2

Chop the rosemary and combine with salt and freshly ground black pepper. Slice a pocket into each of the steaks leaving a ¼-inch margin around the edge. Rub inside and out with seasoning mixture and spread the inside of each pocket with 1 to 2 tablespoons of goat cheese. Place a mixture of red and yellow pepper strips in each pocket and secure with toothpicks.

3

Preheat charcoal grill or heavy cast-iron skillet. Brush steak with olive oil, cook 3 to 4 minutes, and turn. Baste with a small amount of butter and cook an additional 4 minutes. Serve with lemon, boiled new potatoes halved and cooked in olive oil until colored, and baked tomato.

BERRIES ARE A SEASONAL
DELICACY IN THE GREEN
MOUNTAINS. HERE, THEY
ARE ENHANCED WITH A
LIGHT SAUCE AND CREAM.

RASPBERRY GRATIN

LIGHT AND ELEGANT. SERVES 4.

❧

1 pint raspberries
3 egg yolks
pinch salt
¼ cup maple sugar or ¼ cup mixed brown and white sugar
¼ to ½ cup good quality dry sherry
½ cup cream, whipped

1

Preheat broiler. In a stainless steel bowl combine yolks, salt, sugar, and sherry. Whisk over very low indirect heat or in the top of a double boiler until very thick. Place bowl in a large pan of ice water and beat with electric mixer until sauce is cold.

2

Place berries in a shallow baking dish or in individual casserole dishes or ramekins. Spoon sauce over the top and run under broiler until the sauce colors slightly. Serve immediately, topped with a spoonful of whipped cream.

3

An alternative topping is made with sour cream or crème fraîche stirred until smooth, poured over the berries, and sprinkled with maple or brown sugar.

ROSEMARY GRILLED
LOIN LAMB CHOPS WITH
WARM TOMATO VINAIGRETTE

THE WARM TOMATO VINAIGRETTE STANDS ON ITS OWN WITH
ALMOST ANY MEAT OR FISH. SERVES 4.

❦

8 loin lamb chops, 1½ inch thick
4 sprigs rosemary
2 cloves garlic, minced or pressed
2 crumbled bay leaves
salt
freshly ground black pepper
olive oil

1

Two hours before grilling, remove leaves from rosemary sprigs and set aside. Cut rosemary stems in half and use to fasten tail of chop to the meaty part. Rub chops with rosemary leaf, garlic, and bay leaves. Season with pepper and coat with olive oil. Turn several times, working seasonings into raw meat.

2

Prepare a charcoal fire or gas grill. Brush excess marinade off chops and place on lightly oiled, preheated racks. Cook over moderately high heat until well browned. Turn and season with salt and cook over slightly lower heat for 3 to 4 minutes or until the meat feels springy to the touch. Remove to a warm platter. Cover loosely with foil and keep in a warm oven. Top with a little warm tomato vinaigrette or serve on the side.

TOMATO VINAIGRETTE

SERVES 2 TO 4.

❦

⅜ cup olive oil
3 cloves garlic, minced
½ medium onion, finely diced
2 very ripe tomatoes, peeled, seeded, and diced
1½ tablespoons red wine vinegar
1½ teaspoons fresh rosemary, chopped or ¾ teaspoon dried rosemary
2 tablespoons parsley, chopped
1 teaspoon fresh thyme or ½ teaspoon dried thyme
salt
freshly ground black pepper

In a saucepan over medium heat, heat olive oil and add onions and garlic. Cook until onions are soft. Add tomatoes, raise heat to medium-high and cook until they give up some liquid. Add vinegar and simmer 1 to 2 minutes. Add herbs, cook another minute, and season with salt and pepper. Serve warm.

Pasta Salad with Eggplant and Peppers

A GREAT DISH FOR A SUMMER POTLUCK. SERVES 4.

❧

1 cup olive oil
2 medium-sized eggplants, diced to ½ inch
2 red peppers, roasted, peeled, seeded, and cut into strips
2 yellow peppers, roasted, peeled, seeded, and cut into strips
2 medium-sized onions, peeled, halved, and cut vertically into strips
6 cloves garlic, minced
2 tablespoons red wine vinegar
salt
freshly ground black pepper
½ teaspoon fresh rosemary or ¼ teaspoon dried rosemary
1 teaspoon fresh thyme
1 tablespoon fresh Italian parsley
1 pound rotelli
½ cup fresh basil, chopped
½ cup coarse bread crumbs

1

In a heavy skillet over moderately high heat, heat 2 to 3 tablespoons of olive oil and add ¼ cup of cubed eggplant. Cook until colored on one side. Toss gently and cook until just tender and colored. Set aside. Repeat, using 2 to 3 tablespoons oil per batch.

2

Wipe out skillet and heat 3 tablespoons of olive oil over moderate heat. Cook onions until clear and golden. Add garlic and cook until fragrant. Add herbs and vinegar. Simmer until reduced by half. Season with salt and pepper, whisk in additional ½ cup of olive oil. Reserve.

3

Roast peppers over an open flame or under a broiler until the skin is blistered and charred uniformly. Place peppers in a paper bag and close the top. Let steam for 10 minutes to loosen the skin and then peel and remove the seeds and cut into thin strips. Cool.

4

In a 6-quart pot, bring salted water to a boil. Add rotelli and cook until very al dente. Rinse with hot water, drain well, and remove to a large serving bowl. Toss with onion and garlic mixture, basil, and peppers. Gently fold in eggplant and top with toasted breadcrumbs.

MARGARET'S COLESLAW

PROOF ONCE AGAIN THAT TWO HEADS (OF CABBAGE)
ARE BETTER THAN ONE. SERVES 4, TWICE.

1 medium head savoy or other cabbage, trimmed, cored, and finely chopped
1 small head green cabbage, trimmed, cored, and finely chopped
3 carrots, peeled and coarsely grated
1 cup mayonnaise
¼ cup white vinegar
2 tablespoons granulated sugar
salt
freshly ground black pepper

1

In a large mixing bowl, combine cabbages and carrots.

2

In a small mixing bowl, combine vinegar, sugar, salt and pepper. Then whisk in enough mayonnaise to make the dressing the consistency of buttermilk. Pour over cabbage and carrots and mix thoroughly. Let chill, turning several times.

GRILLED CHICKEN PAILLARD WITH SAUTÉED CHANTERELLES

CHANTERELLES ABOUND IN THE VERMONT WOODS IN AUGUST. THEY'RE ALSO OFTEN AVAILABLE AT FARMER'S MARKETS. SERVES 4.

2 to 2½ pounds boneless chicken breasts
1 tablespoon olive oil
salt
freshly ground black pepper
cayenne
4 tablespoons unsalted butter
1 pound chanterelle mushrooms, larger ones cut to uniform size
2 shallots, minced
2 tablespoons parsley, chopped
1 tablespoon chives, chopped
1 teaspoon fresh marjoram or ½ teaspoon dried marjoram
lemon juice

1

Trim fat and place boneless chicken breasts between two sheets of plastic wrap and pound evenly, as thin as possible without tearing. Prepare a charcoal grill. (You can also use a skillet with raised ridges.)

2

In a large skillet melt 3 tablespoons of butter until it foams. Add the mushrooms and toss to coat. Cook until lightly done, tossing occasionally. Add shallots, cook until softened. Add herbs. Swirl in remaining butter and season to taste. Keep warm.

3

Brush flattened chicken with olive oil and season with salt and cayenne. Place on preheated grill or in skillet and cook 20 to 30 seconds. Turn and continue cooking until done, probably another 30 seconds. Transfer to heated plates and top with chanterelles. Serve with couscous cooked with diced red pepper, zucchini, and onion.

WILD MUSHROOMS ADD
GUSTATORY APPEAL TO
GRILLED CHICKEN, A
PERENNIAL BARBECUE
FAVORITE.

CORN AND LOBSTER STEW

HEARTY AND FILLING—THE LOBSTER MAKES THIS A CORN
CHOWDER FIT FOR COMPANY.

—————————————— ❧ ——————————————

1½ to 2 pounds lobster
2 tablespoons butter
2 shallots, minced
1 sprig each thyme and parsley
½ bay leaf
3 cups light cream or half and half
4 ears sweet white corn, kernels removed, cobs reserved
1 tablespoon unsalted butter
1 medium onion, peeled and diced
1 rib celery, peeled and diced
2 medium potatoes, peeled, diced, held in cold water to cover
pinch fresh thyme leaves
salt
cayenne
freshly ground black pepper
1 tablespoon parsley, chopped

1

In a large pot, place the lobster on its back in ½ cup of water. Cover, bring to a boil and steam for 7 to 10 minutes. Remove lobster; shell and reserve as much meat as possible. Cut lobster meat into bite-sized pieces. Break up or coarsely chop carcass. Return pot to heat. Add butter and cook carcass with shallots for 4 to 5 minutes. Add herbs and 3 cups of water, simmer for 30 minutes, and strain. Reserve stock.

2

In a saucepan, combine corn cobs and light cream; bring to a simmer.

3

Return large pot to moderate heat. Add butter and cook onion and celery until onion is clear. Add potatoes and lobster stock. Bring to a simmer and cook until potatoes are tender. Remove corn cobs from cream. Add cream to potato mixture with thyme and lobster meat. Heat just until lobster is heated through and season with salt, cayenne, and pepper to taste.

4

Chowder tastes best if covered, refrigerated overnight, and brought gently back to the edge of a simmer. Garnish with chopped parsley and split, toasted, and buttered Common Crackers.

SWEET PEA AND NEW POTATO CHOWDER

A DUET FOR EARLY SUMMER. SERVES 4.

❦

1 pound new potatoes
1 pound fresh peas, shelled
2 tablespoons unsalted butter
1 medium onion, finely diced
1 quart whole milk
1 teaspoon fresh sage, chopped or ½ teaspoon dried sage
freshly ground black pepper
chopped chives for garnish

1

In a large pot, cover potatoes with cold water. Bring to a simmer and cook until just tender. Drain, cool until easily handled, and dice.

2

In a large soup kettle, heat butter, add onion, and cook gently until clear. Add milk and sage and bring to scalding. Do not let boil. Add shelled peas and cook briefly. Add potatoes and cook until heated through. Season with salt and pepper and garnish with chives.

GRILLED COD STEAKS WITH TOMATO CHIVE BUTTER

THE RICH SAUCE ADDS ZEST TO GRILLED CODFISH. SERVES 4.

---

four 8-ounce cod steaks
2 tablespoons vegetable oil
2 tablespoons olive oil
4 shallots, minced
4 ripe plum tomatoes, cut into chunks
1 tablespoon parsley, chopped
1 cup white wine
2 tablespoons red wine vinegar
1 clove garlic, minced
1 cup butter (plus a little to brush on cod while cooking)
cayenne
2 to 3 tablespoons chives, chopped

1

In a nonstick skillet over medium-low heat, heat olive oil and shallots until softened. Add tomatoes and parsley. Cook for 2 minutes and remove from heat. Purée in processor.

2

In a nonreactive saucepan, over medium-low heat, combine wine, vinegar, and garlic and simmer until 2 tablespoons remain. Add tomato mixture and simmer until thick. Whisk in butter, one piece at a time until incorporated. Season with salt and pepper and add ½ the chives. Set aside in a warm place.

3

Prepare a charcoal fire or gas grill. Season the cod with salt and pepper and brush with oil. Place on lightly oiled rack. Cook for 4 minutes on one side, turn and brush with butter, and cook just until the flesh starts to flake (the fish should be moist and fairly opaque in the center). Put on plates, spoon sauce over cod, and garnish with remaining chives.

Strawberry Shortcake

It doesn't get much better than this.

1 quart strawberries, sliced, a few perfect ones reserved
1 tablespoon sugar
1 tablespoon Grand Marnier (optional)
1½ cups flour
2½ teaspoons baking powder
pinch salt
2 teaspoons sugar
¼ cup butter
½ cup milk
2 tablespoons unsalted butter
1 cup heavy cream, whipped

1

Pick over berries, wash, hull, and pat dry. Slice all but a few and reserve the whole berries for garnish. Sprinkle sliced berries with 1 tablespoon of sugar and Grand Marnier, if desired. Place in a warm spot.

2

Preheat oven to 450°. Sift flour, measure, then resift into a large mixing bowl with baking powder, salt, and 2 teaspoons sugar. Cut in butter until pieces are very small and flour mix has a grainy feel to it. Stir milk into flour mixture until just combined. Don't overwork.

3

Turn dough onto a lightly floured board and roll out a little less than ½ inch thick. Cut out with a biscuit cutter and bake on a sheet for 10 to 12 minutes. Let cool slightly on a rack. Slice horizontally and broil, split sides up, until lightly browned. Butter split sides. Spoon berries over bottom half, place top on with buttered side up and heap with more berries, letting them spill over the edge. Top with a generous dollop of whipped cream and garnish with whole berries.

Ratatouille

A DISH THAT IS MORE THAN THE SUM OF ITS PARTS.

———————————————— ✿ ————————————————

olive oil
2 medium red peppers, cored, seeded, and finely diced
2 medium yellow peppers, cored, seeded, and finely diced
6 cloves garlic, minced
2 small summer squash, finely diced
2 small zucchini, finely diced
2 Spanish onions, peeled and finely diced
8 to 12 plum tomatoes, peeled, seeded, and diced
2 medium eggplants, finely diced, lightly salted, allowed to drain for 20 minutes, rinsed, and patted dry
½ cup fresh parsley, chopped or ¼ cup dried parsley
⅓ cup fresh basil, chopped or 1 tablespoon dried basil
2 tablespoons fresh thyme or 1 tablespoon dried thyme
1 teaspoon fresh rosemary, chopped or ½ teaspoon dried rosemary
1 tablespoon fresh marjoram or ½ tablespoon dried marjoram
2 teaspoons fresh savory or 1 teaspoon dried savory
bay leaf
grated Parmesan cheese (optional)

1

Preheat oven to 375°. In two large skillets add 1 tablespoon of olive oil and heat. When quite hot, add the eggplant, enough to cover the bottom in 1 layer. Cook over moderate heat until evenly colored. Do in batches if necessary, wiping the pan and adding additional oil for each. As the batch is done, place in oven-proof dish. Repeat with peppers. When the color heightens, add the garlic and cook until softened. Remove to dish. Place onions in skillet and cook until translucent. Add squash and cook for another minute, tossing. Remove to dish.

2

Add the tomatoes, bay leaf, and half the herb mixture to the dish. Season with salt. Mix gently but well. Place large dish on stove over low heat and bring to a simmer. Cover, place the dish in oven, bake 15 to 20 minutes or until squash is tender. Remove cover. Add remaining herbs and simmer uncovered (if necessary) to reduce any extra liquid.

3

Adjust seasoning and serve hot, warm, or room temperature. If served hot, sprinkle the top with Parmesan and broil until lightly browned.

CHILLED CANTALOUPE SOUP

A VISUAL TREAT THAT SERVES AS AN UNUSUAL FIRST COURSE OR DESSERT. SERVES 4.

¼ cup sweet butter
2 medium cantaloupes, peeled, seeded, and cubed
pinch sugar
pinch allspice
1 tablespoon grated orange zest
salt
3 cups milk
lemon juice
honey (optional)
1 cup sliced strawberries or 1 cup blueberries, cleaned

1

In a large saucepan over moderate heat, melt butter, add cantaloupe, and cook gently for 2 minutes. Add sugar, allspice, orange zest, and salt and cook, stirring, for an additional 2 minutes. Add milk, bring to a simmer (do not boil), and cook 8 to 10 minutes.

2

Purée in a blender, adjust the flavor with salt, lemon, and honey. Chill soup. Garnish with strawberries, blueberries, or other fruit and serve in chilled bowls.

For those sultry summer days, this chilled cantaloupe soup offers a sweet alternative to gazpacho. Recipe on previous page.

PASTA SALAD WITH SMOKED SALMON

IT'S WORTH THE TROUBLE TO GET FRESH HERBS. SERVES 4.

❧

2 shallots
⅛ cup lemon juice
⅛ cup sherry vinegar
salt
freshly ground black pepper
¾ cup vegetable oil
2 tablespoons fresh dill, chopped or 1 tablespoon dried dill
2 tablespoons fresh parsley, chopped or 1 tablespoon dried parsley
2 teaspoons fresh tarragon, chopped or 1 teaspoon dried tarragon
1 pound pasta shapes (spirals or elbows, etc.)
1 bunch watercress, leaves only
⅓ cup chives, chopped
½ to ¾ pound smoked salmon, cut into thin strips
1 red onion, sliced paper thin
1 hard-cooked egg, peeled, whites and yolks chopped separately
½ cup rye croutons, lightly toasted
sour cream

1

In a small bowl combine the shallots, lemon, vinegar, salt, and pepper. Let stand 10 to 15 minutes. Whisk in the oil and add herbs. Reserve.

2

Cook pasta al dente, drain, rinse with cold water, drain again.

3

In a large mixing bowl, toss pasta with chives, croutons, ½ the smoked salmon, watercress, and enough vinaigrette to moisten. Remove to a low, wide bowl and garnish with red onion, the remaining smoked salmon, and a dollop of sour cream. Sprinkle yolks and whites of hard-cooked eggs over the top and season with freshly ground black pepper.

GRILLED BEEF SIRLOIN, VEGETABLES, AND GARLIC MAYONNAISE

ADD A POTATO SALAD AND CORN ON THE COB
FOR A SUMMER FEAST.

---

2 pounds sirloin steak or boneless short loin steaks, at least 1 inch thick
freshly ground black pepper
2 teaspoons tamari or regular soy sauce
olive oil
1 medium red pepper, cored, seeded, and quartered
1 medium yellow pepper, cored, seeded and quartered
1 medium Spanish onion, peeled and cut into thick slices
8 to 12 large mushroom caps, stems cut, flush with cap
1 small zucchini
1 summer squash, cut on a bias into ¼-inch slices
1 bulb fennel, trimmed, quartered and blanched (optional)
9 new potatoes, simmered until tender, halved
(reserve one for garlic mayonnaise)
1 medium eggplant, cut lengthwise into ½-inch slices
2 tomatoes, halved and seeded

1

Season the steaks with pepper and soy and coat with olive oil. Refrigerate or let sit 2 hours at room temperature.

2

Preheat grill on charcoal fire. Cook steaks on lightly oiled grill racks until well marked on one side, about 4 to 5 minutes, and turn. Cook to desired degree of doneness (another 4 to 5 minutes for rare) and set aside to rest. Clean grill racks and brush the vegetables lightly with olive oil. Grill vegetables, starting with the denser, and add the lighter ones as you go. Cook until tender, remove as they are done, and season with salt and pepper. Cut the steaks into thin slices against the grain and arrange on eggplant slices. Surround with remaining vegetables and serve with garlic mayonnaise.

GARLIC MAYONNAISE

2 egg yolks
1 new potato, cooked, peeled and mashed
4 cloves garlic, minced and mashed to a paste with 1 teaspoon salt, cayenne
1½ cups virgin olive oil
lemon juice

In a small mixing bowl, combine yolks, potato, garlic, and a pinch of cayenne and beat well. Drizzle the oil into the mixture slowly until an emulsion forms. As it gets quite thick, thin with a little lemon juice. Incorporate the oil and adjust the seasonings.

TOMATO SALAD WITH ARUGULA AND BASIL

SERVED WITH BREAD, THIS IS A MEAL IN ITSELF. SERVES 4.

handful arugula (rocket), stems trimmed, washed, and dried
or chopped mixed greens or parsley
2 to 3 pounds ripe tomatoes, washed, cored, and sliced vertically
2 shallots, peeled and minced
2 tablespoons balsamic vinegar
¼ cup virgin olive oil
¼ cup fresh basil leaves, washed, dried, and thinly sliced

Place arugula leaves on a large platter. Lay sliced tomatoes on top. Sprinkle with shallots and vinegar. Season with salt and freshly ground black pepper and drizzle with olive oil. Garnish with basil.

PORK SPARERIBS WITH MAPLE SYRUP AND CIDER VINEGAR BBQ SAUCE

VERMONT SWEET AND SOUR. SERVES 4.

❧

---

3 or 4 sides pork baby back ribs
chili powder
¼ cup unsalted butter
2 medium onions, finely diced
6 cloves garlic, minced
1 cup ketchup
⅜ cup maple syrup
3 tablespoons cider vinegar
1 teaspoon cumin
½ teaspoon coriander
¼ cup basil, chopped
2 tablespoons cilantro, chopped
cayenne

1

Preheat oven to 250°. Season ribs with salt, pepper, and chili powder. Place on wire racks on cookie pans or sheet pans and bake 2 to 3 hours or until the meat is starting to shrink from the bones.

2

Meanwhile, in a large heavy saucepan over low heat, melt butter. Add onions and garlic and cook until very soft. Add remaining ingredients and bring to a simmer. Adjust seasonings and remove from heat.

3

Remove ribs from oven and raise temperature to 350°. Blot ribs with paper towels and coat both sides with sauce. Return to oven and bake until sauce has set, about 15 minutes. Recoat ribs with additional sauce and cook until glaze is set again. Remove from oven, let cool slightly, then cut between each rib.

GREEN BEAN SALAD

THE NUTTY TASTE OF WALNUTS AND THE COMPLEX FLAVORS
OF THIS DISH SURPRISE THE PALATE. SERVES 4.

---

1 head Boston lettuce
1 pound green beans, trimmed
2 tablespoons sherry vinegar or other vinegar
salt
freshly ground black pepper
1 teaspoon Dijon mustard
½ cup walnut oil
1 tablespoon chervil leaf
or 1 tablespoon parsley, chopped and 1 teaspoon tarragon
thin-sliced red onion for garnish
tomato wedges for garnish

1

Separate lettuce into large leaves and gently wash and dry.

2

In a large pot over high heat, bring salted water to a rapid boil. Add beans and cook until bright green and tender-crisp. Remove to a bath of ice water. Chill and drain. Remove to a large mixing bowl.

3

In a small bowl, whisk together vinegar, salt, pepper, and mustard. Add oil slowly to make an emulsion. (Note: for an alternative to walnut oil, prepare the vinaigrette using vegetable oil and then add some lightly toasted chopped walnuts or almonds to the garnish.) Pour vinaigrette over beans to moisten. Serve on lettuce-lined plate and garnish with red onion, herbs, and tomatoes.

GLAZED SALMON SCALLOPINI

THIS RICH AND DELICIOUS GLAZE KEEPS THE SALMON
MOIST AND TENDER.

1 teaspoon olive oil
4 scallions, whites only, minced
1 clove garlic, minced
½ cup dry white wine
1 cup heavy cream
½ cup unsalted butter
1 tablespoon red pepper, finely diced
1 tablespoon yellow pepper, finely diced
2 tablespoons basil leaf, cut into thin strips
1 tablespoon each, parsley and fresh marjoram, chopped
or 1½ teaspoons each, dried
1 pound boned and skinned salmon fillet
1 tablespoon unsalted butter

1

In a nonreactive saucepan over low to medium heat, heat olive oil and add scallions and garlic, cooking gently for 1 minute. Add white wine, bring to a simmer, and reduce until 2 tablespoons remain. Add cream and simmer until quite thick. Turn heat to low and whisk in butter, one piece at a time. Add peppers and bring sauce to the edge of a simmer. Add basil and season with salt and pepper. Set aside.

2

Slice salmon on the bias into ¼-inch-thick slices. Preheat the broiler. Lightly butter 4 ovenproof plates and place on plates so that slices just barely overlap. Sprinkle each with a pinch of parsley and marjoram and thinly layer each plate with sauce. Place under broiler and cook for 2 minutes without turning, or until sauce is browned in spots and fish is just cooked to desired doneness.

BLUEBERRY ICE-BOX PUDDING

A JUST REWARD AFTER A DAY OF WILD BLUEBERRY PICKING, BUT
CULTIVATED BLUEBERRIES WILL ALSO BE FINE. SERVES 4.

⸎

½ to ¾ loaf firm white bread, sliced, crusts removed
1 pint wild blueberries, washed
¼ cup sugar
honey to taste
lemon juice (optional)
pinch freshly grated nutmeg
¼ cup water
1 cup heavy cream
vanilla extract

1

Cut enough bread to fill a rectangular, approximately 6-×-6-inch covered dish in layers.

2

In a large saucepan over moderate heat, bring blueberries, sugar, nutmeg, and water to a boil. (If using cultivated berries add lemon juice.) Simmer berries until they burst but are not mushy. Taste and adjust the sweet/tart level with honey and/or lemon juice. Add enough berries to cover the bottom of the dish. Top with a single layer of bread.

3

Repeat layers of bread and hot berries, making certain each layer of bread is saturated and that no white spots remain. Cover and let cool. Refrigerate overnight.

4

Turn pudding onto a platter and serve with unsweetened whipped cream, flavored with vanilla.

AUTUMN

utumn foliage in Vermont is the most spectacular annual show of color on the North American continent," writes Charles Morrissey in *Vermont: A History*. And I've never heard anyone dispute him, certainly not a Vermonter.

Scarlet, gold, magenta. Carmine. Vermillion. Writers are induced to pull out every color in their verbal palettes in an effort to do justice to Vermont's autumn foliage. It can't be done. Amanda Sessel Legare, a writer who runs a greenhouse in Cabot and who used to work for the state travel division, learned that lesson early. In charge of recording the daily message on the state's Fall Foliage Hotline, she religiously avoided any references to trees "blazing" or "flaming" or, even more to her credit, "Mother Nature's colorful patchwork." Instead, she reported daily on the percentage of leaves that changed color, relying on information phoned in by a cadre of official leaf spotters scattered throughout the state. But even the stalwart Legare found that sometimes the numbers were failing to convey the message. She once recorded a message that said "the foliage is terrific."

COLORFUL HARVEST FOODS ARE MATCHED BY THE RICH COLORS OF A VERMONT AUTUMN ON A MONTPELIER HILLTOP. THE BOUNTY OF LATE SUMMER ENHANCES THE LAST WARM DAYS OF THE YEAR.

"I just couldn't help myself," she apologized later. "It was so pretty out there." Although not a native, Legare is, like many Vermonters, given to understatement.

I have a love-hate relationship with Vermont's foliage. It is so beautiful it unnerves me. I drive around the state, my eyes burning from staring so hard at the hillsides, feeling that I should somehow be able to imprint the vision in my memory for all time. I know from experience that photographs, at least those I take, will not do justice to the display. My memory does not do it justice either. Foliage is a phenomenon that is better in real life than in memory.

For those of us, school age and well beyond, who still live life on the semester plan, autumn paradoxically marks a kind of renewal. It is hard for me to watch as Orion hoists himself over the eastern horizon and to feel that autumnal freshness in the air without thinking of brand-new black-and-white composition books, pristine white paper ruled in blue, newly sharpened pencils, and the feeling of hope that comes with starting a new school year with a clean slate. I hear the dolorous honking of the Canada geese winging south again, and it lifts my spirits to hear the horn of the yellow school bus waiting for tardy children on the back roads.

I'm aware that some people find autumn a depressing time, with all the leaves falling and decaying, flowers dying, and the days growing short. A lot of it depends on how one anticipates winter: with dread of the cruel cold, treacherous roads, and flu or with joy at the prospect of the holidays, the cheer of a warm fire on a cold night, and dusting off the old skis/snow machine/snowshoes.

There is enough going on in autumn to keep one's mind off winter. For those still heating with wood (and more than one-third of the state still does) there is hauling and stacking to be done. Vermonters who keep animals for meat must attend to the slaughtering and freezing of their livestock. Farmers must get in the last cut of hay, chop the corn, ready the barn for winter.

The apple harvest is in and even those who don't grow their own are busy making pies and applesauce, or, my favorite, apple butter. We are lucky enough to own a small cider press and, scavenging wild apples from our own land and our neighbors', we provide ourselves with cider for the year and a great deal of entertainment. Those without their own presses can find custom cider mills, or visit one of the larger, commercial presses for a day's outing.

The final canning, pickling, and freezing of the garden harvest is done in the autumn. Pumpkins must be taken in and made into pie, soup, breads, jack-o-lanterns, and the heads of the scarecrowlike "harvest people" that dot yards and fields.

There are numerous fall foliage festivals and harvest suppers to attend and, if you live in a small town, to bake for and sell raffle tickets at.

The hunter's breakfast is also a popular event in Vermont, attended in the wee hours by those who actually hunt and in the later part of the morning by those who just like to talk about it.

In October, men in camouflage clothing can be seen sporting unwieldy compound bows and snaking through the fields. In November, the deer hunters are of the red-and-orange-coated variety. Their pickups are abandoned at the roadside and the sound of rifle fire fills the air. One learns quickly to wear bright colors during the season and to avoid the woods.

Hunting season brings game and, if you don't bag your own or get some from a neighbor, game suppers. The Bradford Game Supper, attended by more than 1000 people each November, was once called "The Superbowl of Church Suppers" by writer Calvin Trillin. It is hard to imagine another place where a diner can sample at one sitting venison chili, wild boar sausage, moose patties, and paté made of rabbit and pheasant liver.

Some of the best game suppers, however, are less well known: I still consider a meal of snowshoe hare cooked with wine and pancetta and served with polenta at the First Presbyterian Church in Barre a culinary achievement of the highest order. The side dishes served at such meals, whipped turnips and squash, coleslaw and homemade desserts, should not be overlooked, either.

Autumn brings Thanksgiving, with its warmth, good will, and good food. One of my sharpest Thanksgiving memories concerns a friend and fellow writer, Andrew Nemethy, who was in a car accident on his way to a Thanksgiving dinner. The friends who went to rescue Andrew found his car upside down in a ditch off an area of East Montpelier's County Road known locally as the Bermuda Triangle. A picture taken at the scene shows the slightly disheveled but otherwise unharmed driver standing next to his demolished vehicle and proudly holding the pot of mashed potatoes that survived the crash.

The incident gave all of us at least three things to be thankful for. First, Andrew wasn't hurt. Second (let's be honest), it wasn't our car that was lying, totaled, in a ditch. And third, the potatoes were saved. What's Thanksgiving without mashed potatoes?

An Abundance of Apples

1991 was a good year for apples. I know, because we ate bushels of them. We ate them in pies and in applesauce and in applebutter and apple muffins and pancakes. My husband and I and our children and our neighbors and our neighbors' children pressed bushels more into cider, using the small press I was lucky enough to find secondhand. I steamed the wallpaper off the kitchen making cider jelly, and my neighbor Jim Clark and I — two unrepentant moonshiners — have a stash of cider hardening in the cellar.

A good year for apples is a joy for all the senses. In the spring, one gets the visuals: the sight of apple trees in full blossom, the "Degas dancing girls" of Mrs. Appleyard's imagination. In the autumn, the audio component kicks in: there is the sound of apples falling off trees, bonking on tin roofs, thumping with ripe satisfaction to the ground. The cider press squeaks. Bees are in full hum as they hover above the pomace, the apple mash left over from pressing. The scents are there in abundance: the cinnamony smell of applesauce bubbling and pies baking, the sweet rot of pomace, the astringent odor of cider on its way to vinegar. The tastes are too luscious to describe with justice; but you can tell by the smells that apples make for memorable eating.

According to the state agriculture department, there are about 75 commercial orchards in Vermont, producing about 1.2 million bushels of apples in a good year. The majority of these, about 65 percent, are MacIntosh, but other popular varieties include Cortland, Red Delicious, Empire, and Paula Red. At the Farm Show in 1992, a few orchards submitted a total of 40 different varieties, including such oldies as Nonpareil, Wealthy, Twenty Ounce, and Wolf Rivers (once known, I am told, as "boarding-house apples," popular among landladies because a bowl of these large, tough apples could be set out for boarders and remain untouched for a week). Aside from commercial growers, the state has several large-scale commercial cider presses and a handful of smaller custom presses where anyone who arrives with a few bushels of apples can, for a small fee, leave with several gallons of cider.

Ciders can vary almost as much as wines, and cider makers can argue for hours over the combination of apple varieties that will result in a cider with a perfect balance of tartness, sweetness, aroma, and body. About the only thing they will agree on is that 1 bushel of apples makes roughly 3 gallons of cider. Herb Ogden, a former state senator from Hartland whose cider press runs on the same water wheel that powers his stone grist mill and provides electricity for his house, prefers wild apples (those that have never been grafted) to their domesticated counterparts. According to Ogden, these apples are higher in sugar than most cultivars although their tannin content makes them taste "puckery." In the pressing, he says, the tannin is left in the pulp, and the sugar in the cider. My method is to harvest apples from our own few trees (varieties unknown) and beg surplus apples from friends and neighbors. The cider always seems to taste pretty good.

Hard cider was a popular drink in Vermont during the late eighteenth and nineteenth centuries because, without refrigeration and other modern methods of preservation, it could be kept potable for months. Almost every small farm had a small orchard, according to Weston Cate, former director of the Vermont Historical Society, and farmers either ran their own presses or brought their apples to local mills. Leftover pomace was fed to the livestock. Cider that had gone by was used as vinegar. "Most families put up a couple of barrels," says Cate. "You hear of some putting up 8 or 10, but that's probably an exaggeration." Ogden, however, said he knew a man who put up 13 barrels a year, "one for each month and one left over." The man, he said, "died young, at 98."

The hard cider I've made in the past — using a variety of recipes calling for sugar, yeast, maple syrup, and raisins — was barely drinkable, and I won't make any claims for it as an elixir of long life. But I'll keep trying. With luck, next year will be a good year for apples, too.

BEEF AND VEGETABLE STEW

A GREAT TRADITIONAL BEEF STEW. SERVES 8.

───────────────── ❧ ─────────────────

3 to 4 pounds beef shoulder (chuck), cut into large cubes
½ cup flour, seasoned with freshly ground black pepper
¼ cup vegetable oil
2 tablespoons unsalted butter
1 medium onion, diced
1 clove garlic, minced
1 bay leaf
1 rib celery, peeled and diced
water or beef stock or a combination to cover
2 baking potatoes, peeled and finely diced
1 pint pearl or small white boiling onions
1 teaspoon fresh thyme or ½ teaspoon dried thyme
3 carrots, cut into ovals
½ pound green beans, steamed and chilled
½ pound mushrooms, quartered and sautéed quickly in butter

1

In a large dutch oven, heat the oil. Toss half the beef in the seasoned flour to coat very lightly. Shake off excess. Add 1 tablespoon of butter to dutch oven. Over moderate heat, brown the beef and set aside, repeating the process with the second half.

2

Add 1 tablespoon of butter and cook the onions, celery, and garlic until softened. Return the beef to the oven, add bay leaf and cold water or stock to cover. Bring to a simmer and cook slowly for 1½ hours. Add the potatoes, carrots, pearl onions, and thyme and season lightly with salt and pepper. Cook until the meat is very tender and the potatoes have broken up and thickened the liquid. Add the beans and mushrooms and bring to a simmer. Adjust the seasonings and remove the bay leaf. Serve with warm bread or on egg noodles. Garnish with chopped parsley.

Baked Stuffed Smallmouth Bass

An elegant treatment of this abundant game fish.

❧

---

3 pounds smallmouth bass (ocean perch or other mild whole fish may be used
as a substitute) scaled, gutted, fins removed, and rinsed
salt
freshly ground black pepper
⅛ pound slab bacon, diced (optional)
¼ cup unsalted butter
2 shallots, diced
½ pound spinach, washed and chopped
½ pint shucked oysters, chopped, liquid drained and reserved
1½ cups very coarse bread crumbs or cubed day-old bread
2 tablespoons fresh chervil or 1 tablespoon dried chervil
butter for basting

1

In heavy skillet over moderate heat, cook bacon until crisp-tender. Remove bacon to paper towels to drain. Add butter to bacon fat (reduce amount by half) or, if not using bacon, heat butter until foaming. Add shallots and cook to soften. Add spinach and cook until just wilted. Add oysters, mix well, and cook until heated through. Remove from heat, add crumbs, bacon, seasoning, and chervil and mix well. Add reserved oyster liquid if needed to make a moist, loose dressing.

2

Preheat oven to 350°. Season the cavity of the bass with salt and pepper and fill with stuffing. Skewer the cavity closed with toothpicks. Bake on a rack in a baking pan for 10 minutes per inch of thickness at the thickest part of the fish, basting occasionally with butter.

ROAST DUCK WITH CORNBREAD STUFFING

SAUSAGE, NUTS, AND CORNBREAD MAKE AN UNUSUAL AND
TASTY STUFFING FOR THIS HEARTY AUTUMN DISH. SERVES 4.

two 4- to 5-pound ducks
½ pound pork sausage
1 medium onion, diced
2 cloves garlic, minced
duck livers and peeled gizzards, chopped (optional)
2 teaspoons fresh thyme or 1 teaspoon dried thyme
4 cups cubed corn bread
3 or 4 scallions, sliced
2 tablespoons parsley, chopped
1 tablespoon fresh sage, chopped or 1½ teaspoons dried sage
½ cup lightly toasted pecans, chopped
salt
freshly ground black pepper
¼ cup Marsala or sherry wine

1

Preheat oven and roasting pan to 350°. To prepare stuffing: In a heavy
skillet over medium heat, cook crumbled sausage until lightly
browned. Remove to a mixing bowl. Add onions to skillet and cook
until soft and add garlic. Cook for 1 minute and then cook the livers,
gizzards, and fresh thyme. Cook briefly and add to mixing bowl with
corn bread, scallions, parsley, sage, and pecans. Toss well. Season with
salt and pepper and moisten with Marsala or sherry.

2

To prepare ducks: Trim extra fat from neck and inside of ducks. Rinse
and pat dry. Season inside and out with salt and pepper. Stuff and sew
up or truss the birds with wings folded underneath the back. Pierce
the skin with a fork to allow fat to drain while roasting.

Place on a lightly oiled wire rack in the roast pan. Cook for about 2 hours or until juices run clear when the thigh is pierced with a skewer. To brown the ducks further, turn the oven to 500° and roast for 5 to 10 minutes. Remove to a heated platter, cover loosely with foil for 10 to 15 minutes. Remove thread or string and serve with turnips, carrots, parsnips, or sweet potatoes.

BAKED APPLES

VERMONT SOUL FOOD, ESPECIALLY ON A CHILLY EVENING. SERVES 4.

4 medium tart baking apples (Granny Smith, Macintosh, Rome)
¼ cup dark maple syrup
3 tablespoons butter
3 tablespoons maple sugar or 1½ tablespoons white and
1½ tablespoons brown sugar
pinch cinnamon
pinch freshly grated nutmeg

1

Preheat oven to 375°. Wash apples, core, and peel the top third of each. Place in a shallow baking dish and add water and maple syrup.

2

In a small bowl, combine butter and maple sugar and fill the center of each apple. Dust with cinnamon, nutmeg, and brown sugar and bake until tender, basting with the dish juices. Serve warm with vanilla ice cream or whipped cream.

3

For a variation, fill the centers with ½ cup of chopped cranberries and ½ cup of toasted oats before dotting with the butter sugar mixture.

Baked Beets with Orange Vinaigrette

BEETS THAT CAN'T BE BEAT! SERVES 4.

---

8 medium beets, tops trimmed to ⅛ inch long, roots intact
1 tablespoon olive oil
1 crumbled bay leaf
2 teaspoons dried thyme
1 teaspoon dried marjoram
½ teaspoon dried rosemary
1 tablespoon balsamic vinegar
¼ cup fresh orange juice
¼ teaspoon grated orange zest
1 shallot, peeled and minced
salt
freshly ground black pepper
½ cup salad or vegetable oil
Boston lettuce
orange segments for garnish

1

Preheat oven to 400°. In a small bowl, toss beets with oil and herbs. Turn onto a wire rack on a cookie sheet and bake for 40 minutes to 1 hour or until beets are tender.

2

In a large mixing bowl, combine vinegar, orange juice, zest, shallot, salt, and pepper and let sit 30 minutes. Whisk in oil and adjust the seasonings.

3

Remove cooked beets from oven and let cool slightly. Slip off skins, cut into ¼-inch slices, stack, and cut into ¼-inch strips. Toss beets in vinaigrette to moisten and serve on 4 salad plates lined with Boston lettuce. Garnish with orange segments.

BEAUTIFUL FALL FOODS
FROM THE OVEN HERE
INCLUDE BAKED APPLES,
PAGE 59, AND BAKED
BEETS WITH ORANGE
VINAIGRETTE.

Venison with Red Wine Sauce

Elegant camp cookery.

2 pounds venison steaks, at least 1 inch thick
freshly ground black pepper
1 teaspoon dry thyme
2 teaspoons fresh thyme or 1 teaspoon dried thyme
1 clove garlic, smashed
2 bay leaves
3 tablespoons olive oil
2 tablespoons vegetable oil
1 tablespoon sweet butter
1 tablespoon unsalted butter
¾ pound mushrooms, thickly sliced
3 shallots, peeled and minced or 1 small onion, minced
1 cup good quality dry red wine
1 cup beef or veal stock

1

Season the venison with the garlic, 1 teaspoon dried thyme, 1 crumbled bay leaf, and pepper. Coat with olive oil, cover, and refrigerate overnight or for a few hours at room temperature.

2

Prepare the sauce by heating 2 tablespoons of olive oil in a skillet. Add the butter until it foams, then add the mushrooms. Cook over high heat. Add the shallots and cook until the mushrooms are golden at the edges. Add the wine, pepper, thyme, and bay leaf and simmer until there is very little liquid left. Add the beef or veal stock and simmer until lightly thickened. Keep warm.

3

In a second skillet heat the vegetable oil gently and add the butter. Brush the excess marinade off the steaks and place steaks in hot pan. Cook for 4 to 5 minutes or until browned on one side. Turn heat to medium and cook another 4 to 5 minutes, keeping the steaks rare or medium rare. Remove steaks to a warm platter and cover loosely with foil. Pour off any excess fat from the skillet and add the mushroom sauce. Bring to a simmer, scraping up any carmelized particles from the bottom. Remove the bay leaf. Swirl in an additional 1 tablespoon of butter if desired and adjust the seasonings. Pour over the steaks.

WARM LENTIL AND CHARD SALAD

CHEWY AND SLIGHTLY BITTER — A SATISFYING AUTUMN SALAD.

2 cups lentils, picked over and rinsed
8 ounces Swiss chard, washed, dried, and cut into 1-inch pieces
4 tablespoons olive oil
1 medium onion, finely diced
2 cloves garlic, minced
2 tablespoons cider vinegar
cayenne
freshly ground black pepper
1 teaspoon marjoram, chopped or ½ teaspoon dried marjoram
1 tablespoon parsley, chopped or ½ tablespoon dried parsley
2 teaspoons cut chives

1

In a large pot over high heat, bring lentils covered with cold water to a simmer and cook until tender (usually 45 minutes or so). Check for tenderness. Drain.

2

Five minutes before lentils are tender, heat olive oil in a heavy skillet over moderate heat and add onions and garlic and cook until onions are clear. Add chard and cook until wilted. Add warm lentils and sprinkle with vinegar. Toss well and season with salt, pepper, and cayenne. Stir in marjoram. Garnish with parsley and chives.

WARM BEAN SALAD

FILLING AND TASTY, A MEAL IN ITSELF.

———————— ❧ ————————

1 pound chickpeas, Great Northern beans, or other white beans
1 medium onion, halved
1 medium carrot, halved
thyme, parsley, and bay leaf, tied together
salt
1 cup virgin olive oil
4 shallots or 1 medium onion, minced
3 cloves garlic, minced
1 teaspoon cumin
2 tomatoes, peeled, seeded, and diced or 1 cup canned tomatoes, seeded
¼ cup parsley, chopped
4 tablespoons fresh oregano or 1 to 2 tablespoons dry oregano
4 tablespoons lemon juice
1 tablespoon fresh thyme

1

Soak beans overnight, separately if using more than one type. Rinse and in a large stock pot cover with cold water (separately if necessary.) Add carrot, onion, and herbs to each. Simmer until beans are tender but not falling apart. Drain.

2

In a nonstick skillet over medium heat, heat olive oil and add shallots or onion, garlic, and cumin. Cook just until onion is clear. Add tomatoes, parsley, and oregano and remove from heat. Stir and season with salt, fresh thyme, pepper, cayenne, and lemon juice. Pour over warm beans and toss well. Serve in a bowl over shredded or wilted greens.

MUSHROOM BARLEY SOUP

A PERFECT USE FOR LEFTOVER ROAST. SERVES 6 TO 8.

———————————— ❦ ————————————

½ cup barley
4 tablespoons unsalted butter
2 medium onions, peeled and diced
1 carrot, peeled and diced
1 small knob celery root (celeriac) or vegetable celery, peeled and diced
2 medium parsnips, peeled and diced
1 lamb bone with some meat left from a roast
1 quart water and 1 quart beef broth (optional) or 2 quarts water
1 sprig each rosemary, thyme, and parsley, tied
1 cup canned tomatoes, seeded and diced
mushrooms, thickly sliced
2 leeks, white and light green, cleaned and diced
2 tablespoons parsley and 1 tablespoon oregano, chopped for garnish

1

In a large pot, bring salted water to a rolling boil. Add barley and cook until tender. Drain, chill with cold water, and drain again. Set aside.

2

In a large heavy-bottomed pot over medium-low heat, melt 2 tablespoons of butter and add the diced onions, carrot, celeriac, and parsnips. Cook slowly until they start to soften. Add lamb bone, water, and beef broth or water only. Add herbs and bring to a simmer. Cook for an hour or so, skimming occasionally. In a sauté pan over medium-high heat, heat 2 tablespoons of butter until it foams. Add mushrooms and sauté until lightly colored. Add leeks and toss.

3

Remove lamb bone and dice meat. Remove herbs. Add diced meat, tomatoes, and mushroom mixture to the soup and bring to a simmer. Add barley and heat through. Season to taste with salt and pepper. Serve in heated bowls and garnish with chopped parsley and oregano.

Sautéed Stuffed Chicken Breasts

Cordon Bleu with an Italian palette of flavors.

❧

2 large (12 to 14 ounces each) whole, boneless, skinless chicken breasts
freshly ground black pepper
⅓ pound (4 ounces) fresh mozzarella, sliced
2 thin slices prosciutto, cut into strips
1 tablespoon fresh sage, cut into strips
½ cup flour seasoned with salt, cayenne, and ground pepper
1 egg, beaten with ½ cup milk
½ cup fresh fine white bread crumbs
2 tablespoons grated Romano
1 tablespoon fresh thyme
2 tablespoons parsley, chopped
2 tablespoons olive oil
1 clove garlic, peeled and smashed
1 hot chili
lemon wedges for garnish

1

Preheat oven to 400°. Using a sharp boning knife, cut chicken breasts in ½ on either side of the strip of cartilage running down the center. Remove the tenders and trim any excess fat. Slice a pocket in the side of the breast leaving ¼ inch all the way around. Season with pepper and stuff with mozzarella, prosciutto, and sage. Press down to give a uniform shape.

2

In a shallow dish, combine bread crumbs, Romano, thyme, and parsley. Dredge the chicken in seasoned flour, then dip in the egg wash. Let any excess drip off and then coat with the crumb mixture. Place on a wire rack and let sit for 15 to 20 minutes.

3

In a heavy skillet over medium heat, heat olive oil, garlic, and chili. Cook until garlic cloves are lightly colored and remove both the garlic and chili. Place chicken breasts in pan and cook over moderate heat (they will color quickly because of the cheese).

4

Turn the chicken breasts, drain the oil, and place pan in the oven for 5 to 6 minutes or until chicken is done. Serve with a light, fresh tomato sauce and garnish with a lemon wedge.

RICE PUDDING

A SWEET AND SIMPLE DESSERT WITH A LONG AND
HONORABLE VERMONT PAST.

1 quart milk
½ cup long-grained white rice
¼ cup maple syrup
¼ cup granulated sugar
pinch salt
pinch nutmeg
2 tablespoons unsalted butter, melted
½ cup raisins, soaked in tepid water and 1 ounce dark rum (optional)
¼ cup hazelnuts, toasted, skins removed, and chopped (optional)

Preheat oven to 275°. In a large mixing bowl, combine milk, rice, syrup, sugar, salt, and nutmeg. Pour into a buttered 1½-quart baking dish. Bake for 1½ hours, stirring several times to break up the skin on top. Stir in butter, raisins, and nuts, if using, and cook for another 1½ hours undisturbed. Let cool until warm and serve with whipped cream.

SMOKED ROASTED TURKEY

AN AUTUMN AFTERNOON PROJECT WITH A DELICIOUS REWARD.

10- to 12-pound fresh turkey
2 teaspoons salt
1 teaspoon freshly ground black pepper
1 teaspoon garlic powder
pinch cayenne
1 head garlic, split in ½
1 medium onion, thinly sliced
1 sprig each fresh rosemary and sage
2 sprigs parsley
2 ribs celery, with leaves
1 tart apple, cored and sliced

1

Prepare a charcoal or gas grill. When the coals for the charcoal grill are ready, move them to one side away from the turkey, keeping the turkey away from direct heat. If using a large gas grill, place the turkey on one side of the grill and keep the gas going on the other. Add chunks of soaked hardwoods to the charcoal fire or a pan of sawdust on top of the gas burner. Charcoal, hardwood chunks, or pans of sawdust may need to be added during the roasting time.

2

Rinse turkey and pat dry. In a small bowl, combine salt, pepper, garlic powder, and cayenne and season cavity with half the mix. Place garlic, onion, herbs, celery, and apple inside cavity. Tuck wings under shoulder joints and truss legs. Place on a lightly oiled grill rack over the grill. Roast with smoke until the internal temperature of the thigh reads 150° on a meat thermometer. One way to speed cooking and maintain moisture is to place a pan of hot water either underneath or to one side of the turkey during the cooking procedure.

SMOKING AND ROASTING
A SMALL TURKEY TAKES
TIME BUT NO SPECIAL
SKILLS OR EQUIPMENT,
AND THE RESULT IS
DELICIOUS. RECIPE ON
PREVIOUS PAGE.

POTATO AND KALE SOUP

A VARIATION ON A DELICIOUS PORTUGUESE SOUP USING
A PLENTIFUL AUTUMN CROP. SERVES 4 TWICE.

1 tablespoon unsalted butter
1 medium onion
1 pound baking potatoes, peeled and diced
2 quarts chicken stock
½ cup heavy cream (optional)
¼ cup grated Gruyère or Emmenthal (hard Swiss cheese)
1 bunch kale, stems removed, washed, chopped, and steamed
1 tablespoon olive oil
2 cloves garlic
salt
cayenne
crumbled cooked bacon or toasted sliced almonds for garnish

1

In a heavy-bottomed pot over medium heat, melt butter. Add the
onion and cook until translucent. Add potatoes and stock and bring to
a simmer. Cook until potatoes are tender.

2

Remove from heat and purée half the potatoes in a blender with a little
of the stock. Add purée back to the soup pot, bring to a simmer, and
add cream, if using. Remove from heat and whisk in the cheese, a little
at a time.

3

In a saucepan over medium heat, heat the olive oil. Add the garlic and
kale and toss. Season with salt and cayenne. Add to the soup, stir well,
and adjust the seasoning. Ladle into heated soup bowls and garnish
with bacon or almonds.

CURLY ENDIVE CAESAR

A COLORFUL, INVIGORATING SALAD.

1 small head romaine lettuce
1 head curly endive
4 slices sourdough or hearty white bread, crusts removed
2 cloves garlic, peeled
2 cloves garlic, minced
2 tablespoons olive oil
4 anchovy fillets, minced
1 egg, coddled for 1 minute
1 teaspoon Dijon mustard
dash Tabasco
2 tablespoons lemon juice
½ cup virgin olive oil
½ cup freshly grated Parmesan cheese
¼ cup freshly grated Romano cheese
1 red pepper, roasted, peeled, seeded, and cut into thin slices

1

Break the lettuces into medium-sized pieces, keeping the smaller leaves whole. Wash well, dry completely, and refrigerate.

2

Toast the bread lightly under the broiler and, while still warm, rub with garlic cloves and drizzle with olive oil. Dice to ¼ inch.

3

In a small bowl combine the garlic, anchovy, egg, mustard, Tabasco, and ½ the lemon. Whisk until well incorporated. Add the olive oil, gradually alternating with the remaining lemon juice.

4

Place romaine and endive in a large salad bowl. Pour dressing over salad to coat and toss with the croutons and half the cheeses. Garnish with red pepper strips, remaining cheese, and freshly ground pepper.

CRANBERRY TART

THIS RECIPE PROVES CRANBERRIES ARE EVEN BETTER IN
CUSTARD THAN IN TRADITIONAL CRANBERRY SAUCE.
YIELD: TWO 9-INCH TARTS.

sweet cookie dough to line 2 shallow tart pans with removable bottoms
1½ pounds cranberries
½ cup maple syrup
1 cinnamon stick
2 teaspoons grated orange zest
2 cups milk
½ cup sugar
4 egg yolks
1 vanilla bean, cut in ½
4 tablespoons cornstarch
pinch salt
2 tablespoons unsalted butter
1 cup heavy cream, whipped

1

Preheat oven to 400°. Chill dough-lined tart pans in the freezer for 15
minutes. Place a sheet of parchment paper cut to fit inside the pan and
fill with dry beans or rice to weight paper down. Bake for 15 minutes,
remove paper and weights. Lower heat to 350° and bake until done.
Remove and cool.

2

In a saucepan over medium heat combine cranberries, syrup, cinnamon
stick, and orange zest and just cover with water. Slowly bring to a simmer and cook just until the berries burst. Let cool, remove cinnamon
stick, and drain.

3

In a small heavy-bottomed saucepan over medium heat, bring to
scalding 1½ cups of milk, 2 tablespoons of sugar, and the vanilla bean.
Remove from heat.

4

In a small bowl beat the remaining milk and sugar with the egg yolks, salt, and cornstarch until pale yellow. Add a little of the scalded milk to temper the mixture, and then add it back slowly to the milk in the saucepan. Bring back to a simmer and let cook for 30 seconds, stirring constantly. Remove from heat, take out vanilla bean. With thumbnail or the tip of a paring knife, strip into custard all remaining seeds from vanilla bean. Discard shell of bean.

5

Beat in butter then cover with buttered parchment paper and let cool. Fold in the whipped cream into the pastry cream and spread evenly in a thin layer into the tart shell. Top uniformly with the drained cranberries and chill.

INDIAN PUDDING

LIKE DINING AT BOSTON'S DURGIN PARK
WITHOUT LEAVING VERMONT.

1 quart milk
½ cup cornmeal
½ cup dark molasses
¼ cup maple syrup
good pinch salt
1 teaspoon ground ginger
2 to 3 tablespoons unsalted butter
2 tablespoons dark brown sugar
1 egg, well beaten
1 cup milk or half and half

1

Preheat oven to 325° or slightly cooler; warmer temperature may cause separation (wheying). In a heavy saucepan over medium heat, bring 1 quart of milk to a simmer. Add the cornmeal slowly in a stream, stirring constantly. Cook on low heat for about 15 minutes, stirring occasionally. Add molasses and syrup and cook another 5 minutes.

2

Remove from heat and add salt, ginger, butter, brown sugar, and egg. Mix well.

3

Pour in a buttered 2-quart dish and pour the 1 cup of milk or half and half over the top. Bake uncovered for 1½ to 2 hours or until soft. Serve with vanilla ice cream or whipped cream.

PUMPKIN SOUP

THE BRIGHT ORANGE COLOR IS ESPECIALLY WELCOME
AS THE DAYS GROW SHORTER. SERVES 6 TO 8.

one 2- to 3-pound pumpkin, halved and seeded
2 large red peppers, halved, cored, and seeded
2 tablespoons honey
2 tablespoons unsalted butter
2 shallots, sliced
1 carrot, peeled and thinly sliced
2 quarts chicken stock or water
salt
freshly ground white pepper
2 tablespoons olive oil
2 tablespoons parsley, chopped
1 clove garlic, minced
roasted pumpkin seeds

1

Preheat oven to 400°. Brush the inside of the pumpkin halves with honey and place them cut side down on a lightly oiled baking sheet. Split the peppers, core and seed them, and put them on the same pan. Bake until the pumpkin is tender and the skin on the peppers is wrinkled. Peel and dice peppers and scrape all flesh from the pumpkin.

2

In a large pot over medium heat, heat the butter and add the carrots and shallots. Cook until the carrots are starting to soften. Add the pumpkin flesh and cook until most of the moisture is gone and the pumpkin is lightly colored. Add the stock, bring to a simmer, and cook for 45 minutes. Purée in a food mill or blender. Add diced red pepper, season with salt and pepper. Ladle into heated bowls and stir a little olive oil into each bowl. Garnish with chopped parsley and minced garlic or roasted pumpkin seeds.

WARM AND FILLING
SOUPS SUCH AS CREAM
OF ONION OR PUMPKIN
ARE WELCOME IN THE
COOLER, SHORTER DAYS
OF AUTUMN.

CREAM OF ONION SOUP

SERVE THIS WITH ENDIVE CAESAR SALAD AND A LOAF OF
HOME-BAKED BREAD FOR A LIGHT SUPPER. SERVES 6 TO 8.

¼ cup unsalted butter
3 medium Spanish onions, peeled and thinly sliced
2 leeks, whites only, rinsed, thinly sliced, and rinsed again
4 shallots, peeled and thinly sliced
or 1 bunch scallions, whites only, thinly sliced
4 cloves garlic, peeled and sliced
1½ quarts chicken stock or water
2 medium potatoes, peeled and thinly sliced
cheesecloth sachet containing 1 bay leaf, 2 sprigs thyme,
2 sprigs parsley, and 6 peppercorns
1 cup heavy cream
2 tablespoons unsalted butter
salt
cayenne
freshly ground white pepper
scallion tops cut thinly on a bias or chopped chives for garnish
lightly toasted rye croutons for garnish

1

In a heavy-bottomed pot over medium low heat, melt butter. Add onions, leeks, shallots or scallions, and garlic. Cook gently, covered, stirring occasionally until onions are clear and limp. Add stock, potatoes, and sachet and bring to a simmer. Cook just until potatoes are tender and remove sachet.

2

Purée in batches in a blender. Return purée to pot, add heated cream, and bring to the edge of a simmer. Whisk in the butter and adjust the seasoning with salt, cayenne, and white pepper. Garnish with toasted rye croutons and scallion tops or chives.

BROILED PARTRIDGE
(RUFFED GROUSE)

VERMONT'S THRIVING GAME FARMS WILL PROVIDE FRESH
PARTRIDGE IF YOU COME HOME FROM THE HUNT EMPTY-HANDED.
SERVES 4.

---

four 1-pound grouse, dressed and cleaned
2 shallots, minced
½ teaspoon cracked black peppercorns
1 tablespoon fresh tarragon
½ cup dry white wine
2 or 3 small sour gherkins, chopped
3 to 4 tablespoons unsalted butter, room temperature
1 tablespoon whole grain mustard
2 tablespoons Dijon mustard
1 cup coarse fresh white bread crumbs

1

Preheat the broiler and broiler pan. Using a boning knife, cut through the partridges on either side of the backbone and remove it. Using the heel of the hand, gently flatten the bird. Cut a slit in the loose skin of the thigh and slip the end of the drumstick through slit to fasten it.

2

In a saucepan, combine shallots, pepper, tarragon, and white wine and simmer until almost no liquid remains. Let cool, then work in butter. Add chopped gherkins, shape into 4 finger-sized rolls, and chill.

3

Season birds inside and out with salt and freshly ground pepper. Loosen skin on the breasts and place seasoned butter between skin and flesh. Place birds on pan and broil (not too close to the heat) until the skin starts to color evenly and birds are about three quarters cooked, approximately 15 to 20 minutes. Remove the birds and blot any moisture from skin.

Mix mustards and thin with a little white wine. Paint the birds with the mustard mixture. Pat with crumbs to coat the skin side well. Run under broiler to brown and finish cooking until juices run clear when thigh is skewered. Serve with spinach or chard and roast potatoes.

TURKEY STOCK

MAKES 2 QUARTS.

*1 picked-over turkey carcass, or an equivalent amount of
turkey backs, necks, and wings
1 onion, thinly sliced
1 rib celery, thinly sliced
1 carrot, thinly sliced
1 leek, thinly sliced
1 or 2 bay leaves
1 tablespoon thyme, chopped
1 tablespoon parsley, chopped*

In a large pot cover turkey carcass or parts with enough cold water to reduce to 2 quarts stock, adding vegetables and herbs, and bring to a simmer. Skim occasionally and simmer for 2 hours. Strain stock, reserving any turkey meat (no skin or bones) and set aside.

TURKEY GUMBO

FOR THE DAY AFTER THANKSGIVING. SERVES 4 TWICE.

—————————————— ❧ ——————————————

¾ cup vegetable oil
¾ to 1 cup flour
2 medium onions, peeled and diced
1 green pepper, cored, seeded and diced
1 or 2 ribs celery, peeled, and diced
2 quarts turkey stock (see page 79)
1 bay leaf
1 tablespoon fresh thyme or ½ tablespoon dried thyme
½ pound smoked pork sausage cut into ¼-inch quarter rounds (optional)
½ cup canned tomatoes, seeded and diced
1 pound cooked diced turkey meat (can be meat pulled from stock)
salt
freshly ground cayenne pepper
boiled rice
4 tablespoons chopped parsley mixed with ½ cup sliced scallions

1

In a large heavy bottomed pot, heat the vegetable oil until very hot and gradually add the flour, stirring. Cook over high heat for 10 to 15 minutes or until the roux takes on a reddish brown color. Add ⅓ of the onions, pepper, and celery and stir to cook vegetables and cool roux. Set aside.

2

In another pot, bring turkey stock, with remaining onion, celery, and pepper, to a simmer. Whisk in roux a little at a time or until desired consistency is nearly reached. Add leaf and fresh thyme and simmer for 40 to 60 minutes, skimming occasionally. Add tomatoes and sausage and simmer for 10 minutes. Add turkey and simmer until heated through. Skim well. Season with salt, pepper, and cayenne. Serve in heated soup bowls over boiled rice. Stir in a heaping tablespoon of the scallion and parsley mix.

APPLE PIE

THIS RECIPE YIELDS A FAIRLY TART PIE. THE AMOUNT OF SUGAR
COULD BE INCREASED TO MAKE A SWEETER PIE.

❦

pie dough for a two-crust 9-inch pie
5 to 6 cups tart cooking apples, peeled, cored, and sliced
½ cup granulated sugar
2 tablespoons or more maple sugar
pinch salt
¼ teaspoon cinnamon
pinch nutmeg
1 to 2 tablespoons flour
2 tablespoons unsalted butter
lemon juice

1

Preheat oven to 450°. Line a 9-inch pan with pie dough and chill.

2

In a large mixing bowl, combine apples with sugars and spice and sprinkle with flour. Mound apples in the pie pan. Dot with butter and sprinkle with a little lemon juice. Moisten the edge of the bottom pie crust with water and put on the top pastry. Trim and crimp the edges and cut a slit to let steam escape.

3

Bake for 15 minutes at 450°. Lower heat temperature to 350° and bake an additional 30 minutes.

4

Let cool and serve warm with aged sharp cheddar cheese, vanilla ice cream, or whipped cream.

SALT COD AND WHIPPED POTATO CASSEROLE

AN OFTEN OVERLOOKED OLD-FASHIONED DISH.

1½ pounds boneless salt cod
1 sprig each parsley, thyme, and celery leaf, tied
½ medium onion, split
½ bay leaf
1 clove garlic
4 peppercorns
1 pound baking potatoes (2 medium)
2 egg yolks
2 cloves garlic, minced
½ cup milk or half and half, warmed
½ cup olive oil
salt
cayenne
pinch freshly grated nutmeg
2 tablespoons hard grated cheese (Parmesan or Romano)
1 tablespoon chopped parsley
1 hard-cooked egg, peeled and finely chopped

1

Cod should be soaked for 24 hours before cooking. The soaking water must be changed periodically.

2

Preheat oven to 400°. Bake potatoes until tender, keep warm.

3

In a saucepan over very low heat, place cod with the herbs, onion, bay leaf, clove, and peppercorns. Cover with water and heat almost to a simmer. Continue to cook very gently for 8 minutes.

4

Remove cod from the liquid and drain. Remove skin, dark spots, and bones (if any). Separate into small flakes. In a saucepan over very low heat, place half the cod and the garlic with ¼ cup of olive oil. Beat with a mixer until you have a grainy purée. Add the remaining oil alternately with the warmed milk. Keep warm.

5

Scoop the flesh from the potato, mash with the egg yolks, and whip until smooth. Fold in the cod purée, the remaining flaked cod, and season with salt, cayenne, and a hint of nutmeg.

6

Spread into a lightly buttered baking dish or individual shallow casseroles. Sprinkle with cheese, if desired, and run under the broiler to brown. Top with a mixture of the hard-cooked eggs and parsley, and drizzle with a little additional warm olive oil. Serve with garlic toast or croutons.

WINTER

All Vermonters and adopted Vermonters have their favorite Vermont season. If conversation ever flags — and it does sometimes, though Vermonters are less taciturn than is generally supposed — it can always be brisked up by asking a group which season they like best. A surprising number choose winter."

So begins Louise Andrews Kent, a.k.a. Mrs. Appleyard, in *The Vermont Year Round Cookbook*, which she wrote in 1965. Mrs. Appleyard herself diplomatically refuses to play favorites. "Perhaps about seasons she is the same as about her children and grandchildren," she writes, with her habitual use of the third person. "Her favorite is the one she's looking at."

There are good reasons to choose winter. For one thing, a good snowfall makes almost any house — split-level, farm, trailer, or condominium — look picturesque. Snow covers the unraked leaves, broken toys and rusty garden tools, the overgrown garden, and all the flotsam of the times spent outdoors. The ill-stacked woodpile is topped with mounds of snow. The fence posts and mailbox sport peaked white caps.

The landscape is transformed. Apple trees laden with snow look as if they have suddenly burst into midwinter bloom. Graying milkweed pods and brown grasses poke through the drifts in fields crisscrossed with the icy blue tracks of deer, rabbits, fox, and cross-country skiers. One can, as Mrs. Appleyard did, "look over blue-shadowed white fields, over the dark twisting patterns of brooks and rivers to wooded hills beyond that are deep purple furred over with silver. Higher

BRAISED VEAL WITH WINTER VEGETABLES, BROWN BREAD, AND A BUTTERNUT CAKE MAKES FOR A HEARTY WINTER MEAL. IN YEARS GONE BY, VERMONTERS OFTEN ATE PRESERVED FOOD DURING THE WINTER. THAT DIET HAS BECOME BRIGHTER IN THE LAST HALF-CENTURY.

hills are sharply cut in Air Force blue against a pale sky. Higher still the mountains are blue clouds as pale as the sky. They are crested with white that flushes pink at sunset."

Winter has its own sounds: On the roads, one hears the inspiring sound of the plow (saved at last!), the cheerful clinking of car tires encased in chains, the unhappy whining of tires spinning on ice. Snow rumbles off the roof. In the woods, a bluejay shrieks, a clump of snow falls with a cottony thud, branches creak under their burdens, a snow-mobiler roars by.

The season has its own scents: pine tar on wooden skis (the reward for being old enough and old-fashioned enough to still have wooden skis), wood smoke, balsam wreaths, wet wool drying by the wood stove, snowmobile exhaust, burning wool (too close to the wood stove), and holiday baking. Winter is one of the best excuses for baking that exists, if one needs an excuse. It is one of the best excuses for any kind of cooking. There is nothing like a 20-below-zero morning to inspire one to heat up the oven and put the beans in to cook all day.

The winter appetite, honed by days of skiing or snowshoeing or skating, digging the car out of a snowbank, or merely surviving, calls for stick-to-the-ribs menus of meat and potatoes, soup and bread, and desserts that smell like Christmas, redolent of cinnamon and cloves. Ice fishermen—those hardy, sociable souls—are rewarded with a harvest of tasty smelt and chowders of yellow perch and trout.

But even those who choose winter as their favorite season anticipate it with dread. I recall driving down Route 100 in Londonderry with a colleague one stifling August day when he emitted a piercing cry and skidded to a stop. He pointed, I looked: there on the bright-green hillside, a scarlet maple leaf screamed its warning. Despite the heat, I felt a chill wind blow through me. At that moment, I felt no anticipation of the beauty of winter. I thought only of heating bills and dead batteries and getting my children into snowsuits (and out again, minutes later) and lost mittens and frozen, runny noses. It took me a few months to start looking forward to winter: to the transformed landscape and the holiday spirit, sledding with the kids. It took me several months to remember that winter is my favorite season. Or one of them, anyway.

Butternuts

Harry Morse Sr. says butternuts played an important role in his boyhood. "Trying to crack 'em is how I learned to use cuss words," says Morse, a retired dairyman who, with his sons, runs the Morse Farm, a sugaring operation and farm stand atop a scenic hill just outside Montpelier.

Butternuts, a member of the walnut family, can be found in much of the East and Midwest and are prized for their smooth, buttery taste. "I've often thought that the good Lord caused maple and butternut trees to grow side by side on New England hillsides because of the natural and wonderful affinity the product of the one tree has for that of another," wrote Beatrice Vaughan in *Yankee Hill Country Cooking*. "Maple sugar and butternuts belong together, a fact never more evident than in maple butternut fudge, satiny and smooth and the color of a lightly creamed cup of coffee."

Ripening in autumn, the nuts' sticky green husks require gloves for gathering and several months of drying to remove; they are, in fact, ready for cracking just about the time the sap is boiling in Vermont sugarhouses. But it is the rock-hard shell that presents the real challenge. Says Washington County Forester Russell R. Barrett, "It's one tough nut to crack."

To that end, Vermonters have used hammers, anvils, even cars. Some say heat eases the process. Ron Mancini, of Mother Myrick's Confections in Manchester, says he was once offered two bushels of butternuts blackened from burning by an overzealous gatherer. "They were even harder," he reports. One collector who has cracked butternuts since childhood offers this advice: warm the husked nut slightly on a wood stove and set it on its end on a piece of granite. Squeezing the nut along a seam, tap with a 16-ounce hammer. "It may take 20 taps to crack one nut," he said. Fans insist it's worth it.

BUTTERNUT SQUASH AND APPLE SOUP

UNUSUAL INGREDIENTS YIELD A DELECTABLE SOUP.
THE ROASTED SQUASH SEEDS ARE A CRUNCHY, SALTY KICK.
SERVES 6 TO 8.

※

¼ cup unsalted butter
3 pounds butternut squash, halved, peeled, and diced (reserve seeds)
1 pound tart apples, peeled, cored, diced, and sprinkled with lemon juice
juice of ½ lemon
1 leek (white only), finely diced
1 cinnamon stick or ¼ teaspoon powdered cinnamon
¼ cup maple syrup
6 cups chicken stock or water
2 cups cider
roasted squash seeds
freshly ground nutmeg
½ cup heavy whipping cream

1

In a large stock pot over low heat, melt butter and add the squash, apples, and leek. Cook for a few minutes, then add the cinnamon stick and ¼ cup of maple syrup. Cook another 2 minutes. Add the chicken stock and cider and bring to a simmer. Cook until squash is soft. Remove the cinnamon stick, then purée in batches in blender, food mill, or food processor. Return purée to pot and bring back to a simmer. Adjust the tart/sweet balance with additional lemon juice or maple syrup, salt to taste.

2

Garnish with squash seeds that have been washed, dried, lightly oiled, and roasted with a little salt; add a dollop of unsweetened whipped cream, and a few grains of fresh nutmeg.

Red Flannel Hash

ONE OF THE MOST CHEERFUL DISHES TO CROSS
A VERMONT PLATE. SERVES 4.

1½ cups cooked corned beef, finely chopped
1 cup mixed carrots and onions, chopped
1 cup beets, chopped coarsely
3 cups potatoes, chopped
freshly ground black pepper
pinch cayenne
2 tablespoons vegetable oil
½ cup liquid from boiled dinner, or chicken stock, or heavy cream

1

In a large bowl combine beef with onions, carrots, and beets. Season with freshly ground pepper and cayenne to taste and fold in potatoes. In a large nonstick skillet over low heat, heat the vegetable oil. Add the hash to the skillet and pat it down to form a disk that covers the bottom. Cook slowly until the bottom has browned well. Flip in pan or onto a plate and slide back into the skillet. Add the liquid and cook until the bottom is also nicely browned. Serve with poached eggs.

2

Alternatively, preheat oven to 400°. Lightly butter six 6- to 8-inch shallow casseroles and divide the browned hash among them. Pat the hash down and make 2 indentations in each dish. Crack an egg into each depression, run a bead of cream (1 tablespoon per dish) around the edge and bake until the whites are set and the yolks are the consistency of an over-easy yolk, about 5 to 10 minutes.

SAUTÉED CHICKEN BREASTS WITH MUSHROOMS AND MADEIRA

ELEGANT BUT EASY ENOUGH FOR A QUICK WEEK-NIGHT MEAL.
SERVES 4.

2 large boneless skinless whole chicken breasts, halved.
3 tablespoons butter
6 ounces mushrooms, finely chopped
1 shallot, minced or 2 scallion whites, minced
pinch fresh thyme
salt
freshly ground black pepper
soy sauce
1 tablespoon vegetable oil
1 shallot, minced
½ cup chicken stock
1 cup heavy cream
4 tablespoons Madeira wine

1

In a heavy skillet over medium-low heat, melt 2 tablespoons of butter until it foams and add shallots or scallions to soften. Add the mushrooms and thyme and cook until the mushrooms give up their moisture and then reabsorb it. Season with salt, pepper, and soy.

2

Slice a horizontal pocket in each piece of chicken. Divide the mushroom stuffing into four portions and fill each pocket. Flatten out and smooth the edges together. You can fasten the edges with a toothpick.

3

In a heavy skillet over medium-low heat, heat the vegetable oil. Add 1 tablespoon of butter and when it foams add the chicken, placing what had been the skin side down. Cook over moderate heat until lightly browned and turn gently. Cover and lower heat, cook for 4 or 5 minutes or until chicken feels springy. Remove to a warm plate and cover loosely with foil.

4

Pour excess fat from pan and add shallots, cooking until softened. Add ½ the Madeira, the chicken stock, and any juices from the warm chicken. Simmer and reduce to a syrupy consistency. Add the cream and cook until the sauce becomes slightly thick. Add the remaining Madeira and season to taste. Add the chicken pieces, turning several times in the hot sauce. Remove to warm plates and serve.

CHEDDAR FRITTERS WITH
APPLE COMPOTE

SERVE WITH SOUP AND SALAD. SERVES 4.

※

1 cup milk
4 tablespoons unsalted butter
pinch salt
¾ cup all-purpose flour, sifted with pinch of salt
4 large eggs, room temperature
4 ounces cheddar, in ½-inch cubes
4 tart apples, peeled, cored, and cut into eighths
1 cinnamon stick
½ cup sugar
maple syrup and/or lemon juice

1

In a small heavy saucepan over medium heat, bring milk and butter to a boil. Add the sifted flour and stir with a wooden spoon until it forms a ball and pulls clean from the side of the pan. Turn the heat to low and cook a minute longer, stirring. Remove from the heat and let cool slightly. Beat in eggs one at a time, beating well after each addition.

2

Work in cheddar cubes and pipe the mixture from a pastry bag or dollop from a spoon onto a parchment-lined cookie sheet. Cut the parchment into strips with 3 fritters per strip and lower them gently into 350° deep fat.

3

Alternatively, bake the parchment strips for 10 minutes in a 425° oven. Then lower the heat to 375° and bake for 20 minutes. When they are nicely browned, turn off the oven and let dry out a little with the door cracked open.

4

In a heavy saucepan over medium heat, combine the sugar, ½ cup of water, and cinnamon stick and bring to a boil. Add the apples and cook until they are softened but not falling apart. Remove apples to a bowl and discard the cinnamon. Boil down the liquid until syrupy and add a small amount of maple syrup and/or lemon to achieve the desired tart/sweet balance. Serve compote with warm fritters.

BAKED APPLE CRISP

A WINTER FAVORITE.

4 tart apples, peeled and cut into ¼-inch slices,
tossed in juice of ½ lemon
2 cups small white bread cubes or coarse bread crumbs
2 ounces maple syrup
1 cup sugar
½ cup flour
4 tablespoons unsalted butter
½ teaspoon nutmeg
¼ teaspoon cinnamon

1

Preheat oven to 375°. In a large mixing bowl, combine apples, bread cubes, syrup, and ½ cup of sugar and mix well. Place in a buttered 8-×-8-inch baking dish.

2

In a medium-sized bowl, combine flour, ½ cup of sugar, butter, nutmeg, and cinnamon, cutting it together with two knives to achieve a moist, mealy consistency. Sprinkle over the top of the apple mixture and dot with butter. Bake for 45 minutes or until the top is golden brown. Serve with unsweetened whipped cream or vanilla ice cream.

THIS CONTEMPORARY
VERSION OF BREAD
PUDDING BRINGS NEW
TASTES AND FRAGRANCES
TO A TRADITIONAL NORTH
COUNTRY DESSERT.

DRIED FRUIT BREAD PUDDING

PRUNES AND DRIED APRICOTS MAKE THIS BREAD PUDDING
FRAGRANT AND ENTICING. SERVES 6 TO 8.

½ pound pitted prunes
½ pound dried apricots
1 cinnamon stick or pinch powdered cinnamon
pinch allspice
1 small loaf stale French bread, crust removed, sliced,
halved diagonally, and buttered
6 whole eggs
2 egg yolks
1 cup sugar
4 cups half and half
1 vanilla bean, split lengthwise or 1 teaspoon vanilla extract
maple sugar
whipped cream, unsweetened

1

Preheat oven to 350°. In a saucepan over low heat, heat dried fruit and
spices in enough liquid to reconstitute them until soft. Drain and remove cinnamon stick. In a buttered, shallow 9-×-14-inch baking dish,
spread an even layer of the fruit to cover the bottom. Cover with bread
slices buttered side up, laid in overlapping rows. Combine half and half
and vanilla bean with ¼ cup of sugar in a small saucepan and scald.
While the half and half is heating, in a small bowl whisk eggs, yolks,
and remaining sugar until it falls from the whisk in a ribbon. When
cream is scalded, remove the vanilla bean and strip the seeds into the
half and half. Blend the half and half into the egg and yolk mixture
slowly. Pour the custard evenly over the bread slices.

2

Place the baking dish in a larger dish filled with 2 to 3 cups of boiling
water. Bake for 1 hour or until a toothpick inserted into the pudding
comes out clean. Sprinkle the pudding with maple sugar and place
under the broiler to brown. Serve with unsweetened whipped cream.

Mustard Fried Smelts
in Beer Batter

Serve crisp and hot. The mustard lightens
this often oily dish. Serves 4.

2 pounds smelt, cleaned
peanut oil, for pan-frying
1 egg
½ bottle beer
1 cup all-purpose flour
1 teaspoon baking powder
2 tablespoons dry mustard
2 tablespoons cracked mustard seed
1 teaspoon salt
½ teaspoon garlic powder
freshly ground white pepper or cayenne
lemon wedges for garnish

1

In a medium-sized mixing bowl, beat the egg lightly, then beat in the
beer, flour, baking powder, and spices. Beat until smooth. Do not
overbeat. Let stand at room temperature for ½ hour.

2

In a skillet over medium heat, heat ½ inch of peanut oil to 375°. Dip
cleaned smelts into batter. Let excess drain off, then gently place in
skillet. Cook until golden brown on one side. Turn and continue to
cook up to 4 minutes more. Cook in batches and drain on paper towels
as they are done. Serve at once, garnished with lemon wedges.

NEW ENGLAND COD CAKES

TRADITIONAL FLAVORS FOR A WINTER NIGHT. SERVES 4.

&

1 pound boneless, skinless cod
1 pound baking potatoes, peeled and chopped
1 large egg
1 egg yolk
1 teaspoon dry mustard
dash Worcestershire sauce
2 tablespoons parsley, chopped
1 small red onion, finely diced
½ small green pepper, diced
1 tablespoon unsalted butter
2 tablespoons vegetable oil

1

Season cod with salt and pepper and poach or steam until fish just breaks into flakes. Preheat oven.

2

In a medium pot over medium heat, cover potatoes with cold salted water and simmer until tender. Drain, return to pot, and dry out over low heat. Process the potatoes through a ricer or food mill, using the large screen.

3

In a small bowl, beat together egg, egg yolk, and dry mustard. Mix potatoes with egg, yolk, and mustard mixture, add Worcestershire, parsley, red onion, and green pepper. Season to taste with salt and pepper. Gently add flaked fish. Cool mixture.

4

Preheat oven to 400°. Shape into 8 to 10 cakes about ¾ to 1 inch thick. In a large skillet over medium heat, heat vegetable oil and add butter, allowing it to foam, then add cakes. Cook on one side, turn and finish in oven for 5 minutes until lightly colored.

WALNUT AND PRUNE-STUFFED PORK LOIN

THE PRUNES AND PRUNE JUICE ADD A SWEET CHEWINESS TO
THIS DISH AND THE SAUCE BECOMES ALMOST A GLAZE.
SERVES 4.

2 pounds boneless center cut pork loin
2 cloves garlic, peeled and cut into slivers
salt
freshly ground black pepper
poultry seasoning
½ cup walnuts, coarsely chopped
1 cup pitted prunes
1 tablespoon butter
1 tablespoon vegetable oil
2 tablespoons bourbon whiskey
½ cup unsweetened prune juice
1 cup veal or chicken stock

1

Preheat oven and roasting pan to 325°. Cut slits in pork loin just under
the fat and slide in garlic slivers. With a long, sharp knife cut a hole in
the center of the eye of the loin from one end to the other.

2

In a small bowl, combine prunes and walnuts and stuff into pork loin.
Tie pork roast to help keep its shape during roasting and season outside with salt, pepper, and poultry seasoning.

3

In a large cast-iron skillet or Dutch oven over medium heat, add vegetable oil and butter. Let butter foam then add the pork roast. Cook
over medium heat and brown evenly on all sides. Remove roast and
place on rack in preheated roasting pan. Roast pork until it reaches an

internal temperature of 145°. Place on a warm platter and cover loosely with foil. Let rest a minimum of 20 minutes while you prepare sauce.

4

Pour off any excess fat from drippings and remove from heat. Add the bourbon. Scrape up any caramelized drippings from the skillet with a wooden spoon and let the alcohol evaporate as liquid reduces. Add the prune juice and veal stock (or bouillon cube and water) and simmer to reduce by one third the original volume. If you like a thicker sauce, add 1 tablespoon of arrowroot to 2 tablespoons of cold water and stir into the simmering sauce. Bring to a gentle boil for about 15 seconds or until sauce clears somewhat and is thickened.

5

Remove strings, slice pork, and serve overlapping on hot plates with the bourbon sauce.

SCALLOPED OYSTERS

A LINK TO VERMONT'S LONG TRADITION
OF OYSTERS ON CHRISTMAS EVE. SERVES 4.

⅜ cup unsalted butter
2 tablespoons olive oil
1 clove garlic, minced
½ cup Common Cracker crumbs
½ cup fresh bread crumbs, coarse
2 tablespoons parsley, chopped
2 tablespoons cut chives or scallion tops
pinch oregano
2 pints shucked oysters with their liquid
salt
freshly ground black pepper
cayenne
lemon wedges

1

Preheat oven to 400°. Rid oysters of any shell fragments. Drain well and reserve the liquid.

2

In a heavy saucepan over low heat, heat butter and olive oil together. When the butter foams, add the garlic and cook gently until softened. Add the cracker crumbs, bread crumbs, parsley, chives, and oregano. Remove from heat and add enough oyster liquid to moisten. Season.

3

Butter 4 individual casserole dishes and divide ½ the crumb mixture among them. Add the oysters to the casserole and cover with a thin layer of crumb mixture. Dot with butter and place in the oven. Bake for 10 minutes or until the casseroles are bubbling around the edges. Broil to brown the top and finish cooking. Cook just until the oysters are plump and start to curl at the edges. Serve with lemon wedges.

PASTA FOR A VERMONT
WINTER'S EVENING:
MOSTACCIOLI WITH A
PEPPER-RICH, FRAGRANT
TOMATO SAUCE. RECIPE
ON FOLLOWING PAGE.

Mostaccioli with Italian Sausage and Peppers

LONG A STAPLE OF BARRE ETHNIC CUISINE, THIS RECIPE ADDS A
FEW COLORFUL AND PLEASANT SURPRISES. SERVES 4.

---

1 pound hot or sweet Italian sausage
2 tablespoons olive oil
2 medium onions, peeled and thinly sliced
2 medium red peppers, cored, seeded, membrane removed,
cut into thin 1-inch-long strips
2 medium green peppers, cored, seeded, membrane removed,
cut into thin 1-inch-long strips
6 cloves garlic, minced
1 tablespoon fennel seeds
1 teaspoon dried chili flakes, optional
Two 10-ounce cans tomatoes, drained, seeded, and diced,
juice reserved
⅓ cup Italian or curly parsley, chopped
2 tablespoons fresh basil or 3 teaspoons dried basil
1 pound mostaccioli (penne rigate) cooked al dente, drained, and cooled
3 tablespoons unsalted butter
½ cup grated Parmesan or Romano
salt
freshly ground black pepper

1

Preheat oven to 350°. Remove sausage from casings and cut into
chunks. In a cast-iron skillet over low heat, brown sausage and render
out fat. Remove sausage and drain on paper towels.

2

Add olive oil and 2 tablespoons of sausage fat to skillet and heat. Add
onions and cook until golden. Add peppers and garlic and cook until
peppers are brightly colored and garlic is softened. Add fennel seed,

chili flakes, and tomatoes plus juice and bring to a simmer. Add sausage and cook for 5 minutes.

3

Combine sausage and pepper mixture, pasta, herbs, and 2 tablespoons of unsalted butter. Toss well and adjust seasoning. Pour in buttered casserole or baking dish and top with grated cheese and dot with remaining butter. Bake until heated through and browned on top.

SAUTÉED WALLEYE WITH BUTTERNUTS

An easy, beautiful, and tasty way to serve game fish.
Serves 4.

four 6- to 8-ounce walleye or perch fillets
½ cup flour seasoned with salt and pepper
2 tablespoons peanut or vegetable oil
1 whole lemon, peeled, seeded, cut into segments and diced,
juice reserved
4 tablespoons lightly toasted butternuts or almonds
2 tablespoons parsley, chopped
4 tablespoons unsalted butter

1

In heavy skillet over medium heat, heat peanut oil until quite hot. Dredge fish in seasoned flour, patting off excess. Place in skillet skinned side up and cook until well browned. Gently turn and continue cooking until done. Put fish on a plate, top with diced lemon, and keep warm.

2

Pour excess oil from pan and wipe. Heat butter in the pan until foaming and brown. Add lemon juice, butternuts, and chopped parsley and pour mixture over fillets.

VERMONT CHEDDAR AND ALE SOUP

VERMONT'S MOST FAMOUS CHEESE COMBINED WITH VERMONT'S
MOST FAMOUS BEER. SERVES 6 TO 8.

¼ cup unsalted butter
1 medium onion, diced
2 medium carrots, diced
1 white leek, diced
2 shallots, finely diced or 4 scallion whites
4 tablespoons all-purpose flour
1 bottle Catamount Gold ale (or Amber or Porter)
1 cup heavy cream
1 cup grated sharp cheddar cheese
1 teaspoon Worcestershire sauce
1 tablespoon Dijon mustard
salt
cayenne
rye croutons
2 tablespoons Parmesan cheese, grated
4 tablespoons parsley, chopped

1

In a heavy-bottomed pot over low heat, melt the butter. Add the vegetables and cook gently, covered, for 5 minutes or until vegetables are softened. Dust the vegetables with the flour and continue cooking for 3 or 4 minutes or until the flour has become very lightly colored. Remove from heat and cool.

2

Mix the ale with 2 quarts of water. Heat gently. Whisk ale mixture in the vegetables and bring to a simmer. Simmer for 30 minutes and remove from heat. Cool until just warm and carefully process in a blender, food processor, or food mill.

3

Return purée to pot. Add the cream and bring to a simmer. Whisk in the cheddar cheese gradually. Do not boil. When all the cheddar is incorporated, whisk in the Worcestershire and Dijon. Season to taste.

4

Toast ½ cup of ¼-inch rye croutons with one tablespoon of melted butter until lightly colored, then tossed with 2 tablespoons of grated Parmesan and 4 tablespoons of chopped parsley. Ladle soup into warm cups or bowls and garnish with rye croutons and chopped parsley.

TARTAR SAUCE

SERVING: 1½ CUPS.

1 cup mayonnaise
1 tablespoon Dijon mustard
2 tablespoons parsley, chopped
2 tablespoons red onion, finely diced
2 tablespoons sour gherkins (cornichons), chopped
2 tablespoons capers, rinsed, drained, and chopped
1 tablespoon fresh dill (optional)
lemon juice
Tabasco

In a small mixing bowl, combine all ingredients and mix well. Add lemon juice and Tabasco to taste.

PAN-FRIED PERCH WITH
TARTAR SAUCE

CAYENNE PEPPER MAKES PLAIN PERCH MORE SPRIGHTLY.
SERVES 2 TO 4.

2 pounds perch, cleaned
milk
dash Tabasco
½ cup flour
½ cup corn flour or extra fine cornmeal
salt
freshly ground black pepper
cayenne
peanut oil or vegetable oil for deep frying
tartar sauce (see page 105)
lemon wedges for garnish

1

In a shallow bowl, cover perch with milk and dash of Tabasco and stir. Refrigerate, covered, for at least 1 hour.

2

In a cast-iron skillet over medium heat, heat peanut oil to 350°. (Oil should be ¾ inch deep.) While oil is heating, combine flour, corn flour, salt, pepper, and cayenne to taste in a paper bag or flat baking dish. Remove the perch 3 or 4 at a time from the milk and shake or roll to coat well. Slide gently into hot oil and cook until golden on one side. Turn and continue to cook up to 4 minutes. Cook in batches and drain on paper towels as they are done. Keep warm and serve with lemon wedges and homemade tartar sauce.

BEEF, BEER, AND ONION STEW

DARK, RICH, AND FLAVORFUL. SERVES 4.

———————————— ❧ ————————————

2 pounds boneless beef chuck, bottom round, or top butt,
cut into ¾-inch slices, 2 to 3 inches long
3 or 4 slices lean country-style bacon, cut into ¼-×-1-inch strips
1½ pounds onions, peeled and sliced
2 tablespoons unsalted butter
4 cloves garlic, minced
2 tablespoons balsamic vinegar
1 tablespoons fresh thyme or 1½ teaspoons dried thyme
1 bay leaf
1 teaspoon Worcestershire sauce
2 tablespoons maple syrup
1 bottle dark beer (Catamount Porter or Guinness Stout)
1 cup veal stock
2 tablespoons Dijon mustard
chopped chives for garnish

1

Preheat oven to 325°. In a cast-iron skillet over low heat, cook bacon until lightly browned. Remove to large casserole or Dutch oven. Add the butter to the bacon fat in the skillet and heat until it foams. Season the beef with salt and pepper and brown over moderately high heat. Remove to a Dutch oven.

2

Add the onions to the skillet and cook until translucent. Add the garlic and cook until softened. Add the vinegar and simmer for 1 minute. Add the thyme, bay leaf, Worcestershire sauce, maple syrup, porter, and veal stock and bring to a simmer. Pour over beef, cover, and simmer very gently or braise in oven for 1 to 2 hours or until beef is tender. Remove the beef to a serving dish. Simmer the remaining liquid until it has reached the consistency you desire, skimming the fat from the surface. Whisk in the mustard and adjust the seasoning. Serve over egg noodles and garnish with chopped chives.

WHITE BEAN AND SMOKED HAM SOUP

SERVE WITH BREAD AND SALAD. SERVES 6 TO 8.

¼ cup unsalted butter or bacon fat
1 medium onion, finely diced
2 carrots, finely diced
1 rib celery, peeled and finely diced
1 leek, white and light green, finely diced
1 pound white beans, rinsed,
soaked overnight in water to cover by 4 inches
2 or 3 ham hocks or 8-ounce slab country bacon
(if using bacon instead of ham hocks, dice and render out the fat
in a heavy-bottomed pot; set aside bacon pieces)
Tie together: 1 bay leaf, 1 sprig rosemary, and 2 sprigs parsley
salt
cayenne
1 bunch scallions, tops and bottoms sliced
½ teaspoon rosemary combined with ⅓ cup chopped parsley

1

In a 4-quart stock pot over low heat, melt butter and add vegetables. Stir to coat. Add drained beans and ham hocks (or diced, rendered bacon) and stir. Add herb bouquet and water to cover and cook until beans are tender.

2

Remove ham hocks and peel and dice meat. Add back to the pot. With a spoon, mash some of the beans against the side of the pot to thicken. Bring to a simmer. Add salt and cayenne to taste.

3

Stir in the scallions and rosemary-parsley mixture and ladle at once into hot cups or bowls. This soup is also good served over cooked rice.

BROWN BREAD TURNS
WHITE BEAN AND
SMOKED HAM SOUP INTO
A TRADITIONAL MEAL.
WHITE WINE AND A SALAD
UPDATE IT NICELY.

BROWN BREAD

FOUR FLOURS (COUNTING THE CORNMEAL) GIVE THIS BREAD
TEXTURE, FLAVOR, AND LOTS OF NOURISHMENT.
SERVING: 1 OR 2 LOAVES.

1 cup raisins
½ cup all-purpose flour
½ cup whole wheat flour
½ cup rye flour
½ cup cornmeal
1½ teaspoons baking soda
¾ teaspoon salt
½ cup chopped black or regular walnuts
½ cup molasses
1¼ cup buttermilk
2 tablespoons melted butter

1

In a small bowl, toss raisins with a couple of tablespoons of all-purpose flour and set aside. In a large bowl, mix remaining dry ingredients thoroughly.

2

In a small bowl combine the molasses, butter, milk, and melted butter. Stir gradually into the dry ingredients. Fold in the raisins and walnuts and pour into a buttered loaf pan, two 1-pound coffee cans, or tin molds. Fill the molds a bit more than half full, cover tightly with buttered foil or parchment.

3

Place on a wire rack or trivet in a large steaming pot and add boiling water to the mid-point of the molds. Steam on stove for 2 to 3 hours, depending on the size of the mold(s). Remove to a rack to cool slightly. Remove from molds.

Halibut Baked in Parchment

A jazzy presentation; the fish comes to the table
steaming hot. Serves 4.

※

1½ pounds halibut, flounder or
other white-fleshed fish fillet, cut into eight 3-ounce slices
1 tablespoon unsalted butter
salt
cayenne
1 lemon, peeled, seeded, sectioned, and cleaned of membrane,
juice reserved
1 tablespoon chives, chopped
1 tablespoon fresh tarragon or 1 teaspoon dry tarragon
foil or parchment paper
vegetable oil

1

Preheat oven to 400°. Cut four heart-shaped pieces of foil or parchment (large enough to fit 2 pieces of halibut plus 2 inches all around) and fold in the middle. Unfold and butter parchment where halibut will lie and on the opposite side (not around edges). Set halibut slices (2 per packet) barely overlapping on parchment and season with salt and cayenne. Place 2 or 3 lemon segments on the halibut, sprinkle with a small amount of juice and the chives and tarragon. Seal parchment by folding top over and making a series of small folds all the way around the heart.

2

In a large skillet, heat vegetable oil. Place the packages two at a time in the skillet and heat until they puff. Slide onto a baking sheet and place in oven. Cook for 6 to 7 minutes (total cooking time should be just under 10 minutes per inch of thickness at the thickest part of fillet).

3

Slide packages onto heated dinner plates and let each person open their own at the table.

Ice-fishing Chowder

A WARM FINISH TO A COLD DAY. SERVES 6 TO 8.

2 pounds skinless, boneless fillets, pike or walleye
1 bay leaf
1 tablespoon fresh thyme or 1½ teaspoons dried thyme
¼ pound salt pork or ¼ cup bacon fat
2 medium onions, peeled and diced
1 rib celery, peeled and diced
4 tablespoons flour
3 potatoes, peeled and diced, covered with cold water and
simmered until just tender
1 quart half and half, warmed
2 tablespoons parsley, chopped
2 tablespoons chives, chopped
¼ cup butter, chilled and cubed
Common Crackers for garnish

1

In a small pot bring one quart of water, bay leaf, and thyme to a simmer. Add fish and cook until fish can just be broken into chunks with a fork. Remove fish and break up into chunks, reserving liquid.

2

In a skillet over low heat, heat render salt pork, or heat bacon fat, then add onions and celery, cooking until softened. Dust with flour and cook, stirring until ivory-colored. Whisk in reserved fish liquid and simmer 20 minutes.

3

Add potatoes, fish, and heated half and half and bring back to a simmer. Do not boil. Add parsley and chives and adjust seasonings.

4

Ladle into cups or bowls and garnish with butter cubes and split, toasted, and buttered Common Crackers.

HAM AND SPINACH FRITTATA

COOK THIS IN A CAST-IRON SKILLET AND BRING PAN AND ALL
TO THE TABLE FOR A STYLISH PRESENTATION. SERVES 4.

---

3 tablespoons unsalted butter
¼ pound maple or cob smoked ham, diced
1 clove garlic, minced
¾ cup cooked spinach, chopped and well-drained
1 tablespoon fresh sage or 1½ teaspoons dried sage
8 large eggs
2 tablespoons warm water
dash hot pepper sauce (Tabasco style)
1 red pepper, roasted, peeled, seeded, and cut into strips
½ cup mild cheddar cheese
2 tablespoons grated Romano or Parmesan cheese
salt
freshly ground black pepper

1

Preheat broiler. In a 10-inch cast-iron skillet over low heat, heat butter. Add ham and garlic and cook gently until fragrant. In a small bowl, whisk eggs with drained spinach, sage, warm water, and pepper sauce; pour over ham and garlic. Cook, stirring until eggs begin to stiffen. Shape egg mass into disk of even thickness. Place red pepper strips on top and cover with lacy web of grated cheddar. Sprinkle with Romano and place under broiler. Cook until puffed and golden.

2

Loosen frittata with a spatula and slide onto a heated platter. Season with salt and freshly ground pepper. Serve with potatoes and toast.

BOILED DINNER

AN UNBEATABLE NEW ENGLAND TRADITION! SERVES 8.

※

one 4- to 5-pound corned-beef brisket
1 head garlic (split garlic and with a whole clove,
fasten a bay leaf to one of the halves)
15 medium potatoes covered with cold water,
simmered until tender, and peeled
15 beets, unpeeled with the root end and ¼ inch of the tops left on
1 tablespoon olive oil
freshly ground black pepper
thyme
1½ cups sour cream
3 tablespoons finely grated horseradish
6 carrots, peeled and chopped
6 parsnips, peeled and chopped
3 turnips, peeled and chopped
2 heads savoy or other cabbage, cored and quartered
3 tablespoons parsley, chopped
2 tablespoons chives, chopped
2 quarts chicken stock
1 pint pearl onions or 12 white boiling onions,
peeled with an × cut in the root end

1

Preheat oven to 400°. Rinse the brisket and place in a large pot with the garlic halves and water to cover by 2 inches. Bring to a simmer, skimming frequently. Cook gently (weighted down if necessary) for about 3 hours, or until tender.

2

In a shallow pan, toss beets with olive oil, pepper, and thyme and bake on a wire rack for 40 minutes to 1 hour or until tender. Remove skins and set beets aside.

3

Mix together sour cream and horseradish. Purée one beet. Swirl purée in sour cream and horseradish mixture to achieve a marbled effect.

4

In a large stock pot, simmer chicken stock. Add cabbage and cook until tender yet crisp. Drain and set stock aside. Add the trimmed carrots, parsnips, and turnip to the corned beef during the last 30 minutes of simmering and the pearl onions in the last 20 minutes. Add the cooked potatoes and cabbage to reheat at the very end.

5

Reheat the chicken stock and add the baked beets to heat through.

6

When the beef and vegetables are tender, remove to a warmed platter and moisten with some of the simmering liquid. Serve with the sour cream and horseradish sauce and a mix of 2 tablespoons of sweet butter whisked into the cooking liquid in a heated bowl. Garnish with chopped chives and parsley.

CORNED BEEF, POTATOES,
AND WINTER VEGETABLES
ARE A TIME-HONORED
COMBINATION. ENJOYING
A BOILED DINNER NOW
AND THEN REMINDS ONE
OF THE TASTINESS OF
TRADITIONAL FOODS.
RECIPE ON PREVIOUS
PAGE.

TOURTIERE

A SPICY AND FRAGRANT INTRODUCTION TO
FRENCH-AMERICAN CUISINE. SERVING: ONE 9-INCH PIE.

❦

3 tablespoons butter
⅛ pound slab bacon or salt pork, diced
1 onion, diced
2 cloves garlic, minced
1 pound ground veal or finely chopped veal strip (neck) or turkey
1 pound ground pork or finely chopped pork butt (shoulder)
2 tablespoons water
salt
freshly ground black pepper
freshly grated nutmeg
½ cup fresh bread crumbs or 2 or 3 Common Crackers, crushed
pie dough for a double-crust 9-inch pie

1

Preheat oven to 400°. In a cast-iron skillet over low heat, melt butter. Add slab bacon and cook gently to render fat and brown. Add onion and garlic and cook until onion is clear and garlic softened. Mix pork and veal and add to skillet. Cook for 10 minutes, stirring. Add water, seasonings, and cracker crumbs and mix well. Remove from heat.

2

Line a pie pan with the dough. Fill with the meat mixture and cover with the top crust. Press edges together with your fingers or a fork and cut a few slits in the top to vent the steam. Bake for 40 minutes, remove from oven, and let sit for 15 minutes. Serve hot or cold.

3

Alternatively, roll out dough and cut circles 5 inches in diameter. Fill one side, moisten the edges with water, and fold over to make a turnover. Crimp edges with a fork and bake for 30 minutes.

GRILLED CHICKEN AND WATERCRESS SALAD

A DELIGHTFUL LUNCHEON. SERVES 4.

❧

salt
freshly ground black pepper
olive oil to coat
2 whole chicken breasts, boneless and skinless
2 teaspoons Dijon mustard
3 tablespoons balsamic vinegar or red wine vinegar
1 tablespoon fresh tarragon or 1½ teaspoons dried tarragon
½ cup olive oil
½ cup peanut or vegetable oil
2 bunches watercress, large stems removed, washed, and dried
one 8-ounce package alfalfa/radish/sprout mixture
large lettuce leaves to line plates
2 tablespoons unsalted butter
½ pound shiitake or cultivated mushrooms, thinly sliced
1 clove garlic, minced
2 tablespoons parsley, chopped
½ teaspoon soy sauce
pinch sugar

1

To prepare chicken: Using a sharp knife, cut in ½ on either side of cartilage strip running down the center. Season with salt and pepper and brush with olive oil. In a cast-iron skillet or on an indoor grill, cook over moderate heat. Cook until nicely colored on one side and turn. Cook until just done. Set aside to cool to room temperature. Shred into thin strips with your hands.

2

To prepare vinaigrette: In a small bowl, combine vinegar, tarragon, mustard, salt, and pepper. Whisk together and drizzle olive and peanut oils slowly in a thin stream. Adjust seasoning. Pour over chicken, add watercress, and toss to coat.

3

In a sauté pan or small skillet over medium heat, melt butter. Add mushrooms. Cook until browned, stirring occasionally. Add garlic and cook until softened. Add parsley, then remove from heat and add salt, soy, and sugar to taste. Mix well.

4

Line plates with large lettuce leaves. Rim the plate with sprouts and place chicken and watercress in the center. Scatter mushrooms over chicken and season with freshly ground pepper.

BRAISED VEAL SHANK WITH WINTER VEGETABLES

ASK YOUR BUTCHER TO PREPARE THE VEAL FOR THIS HEARTY
STEW-LIKE DISH. SERVES 4.

four 8-ounce veal shanks, crosscut into 1½-inch slices
3 tablespoons olive oil
2 tablespoons unsalted butter
2 leeks, white and light green, finely diced
2 carrots, peeled and finely diced
2 parsnips, peeled and finely diced
2 medium onions, peeled and finely diced
one 10-ounce can whole tomatoes, drained, seeded, and diced
1 cup white wine
1 cup veal stock
1 bay leaf
1 tablespoon thyme or 1½ teaspoons dried thyme
½ cup parsley, chopped, mixed with
1 tablespoon grated orange zest
4 cloves garlic, minced
salt
freshly ground black pepper

1

Preheat oven to 325°. In large heavy skillet, heat olive oil over medium heat. Season shanks with salt and pepper. When oil is quite hot but not smoking, add shanks and cook over medium heat until brown on both sides. Remove to heavy casserole dish or dutch oven.

2

Lower heat, add butter, and when butter foams, add carrots, parsnips, onions, and leeks. Cook until vegetables start to soften. Add tomato, white wine, and veal stock. Cook, stirring to scrape bottom with a wooden spoon, until liquid simmers.

Add bay leaf. Cover and bake in oven for 1½ hours. Add thyme and bake until shanks are very tender, another 30 to 60 minutes. Remove shanks to a heated serving platter. Simmer liquid with half of the parsley mixture to achieve a fairly thick sauce. Pour over shanks and garnish with remaining parsley mixture.

4

Serve with boiled buttered rice mixed with peas, sautéed mushrooms, and Parmesan, or with egg noodles.

PARSNIP AND APPLE SLAW

MAKES YOU WISH COCONUTS GREW IN VERMONT.
SERVES 8 TO 12.

1 pound parsnips, peeled and grated
2 pounds tart apples, peeled, cored,
and rubbed with a cut lemon, then grated
1 cup maple yogurt or
1 cup plain yogurt and 2 tablespoons maple syrup
2 tablespoons cider vinegar
1 tablespoon honey
1 tablespoon fresh ginger, grated or 1½ teaspoons powdered ginger
2 tablespoons shredded coconut, toasted lightly

1

In a large bowl, combine parsnips and apples.

2

In a small bowl, combine grated ginger and vinegar and let stand 10 minutes. Add yogurt and honey and mix. Pour over parsnips and apples and toss to coat. Top with toasted coconut.

TURKEY POT PIE

PUFF PASTRY MAKES AN UNCONVENTIONAL TOPPING
FOR THIS POT PIE. SERVES 4.

1½ pounds cooked turkey meat
2 cups turkey broth or chicken stock
12 pearl onions or 6 white boiling onions, peeled,
with an ✕ cut in the root end
3 carrots, peeled and cut into uniform ovals 1 inch long
5 tablespoons unsalted butter
1 cup mushrooms (cultivated, oyster, or shiitake), thickly sliced
1 clove garlic, minced
½ teaspoon fresh thyme or pinch dried thyme
salt or soy sauce
½ cup frozen peas, thawed and drained
3 tablespoons all-purpose flour
¾ cup heavy cream
cayenne
few drops of lemon juice
biscuit dough or puff pastry rolled out thick to cover

1

In a large pot over medium heat, add onions and carrots to the stock and cook until barely tender. Set aside.

2

In a skillet over medium heat, melt 2 tablespoons of butter and when it foams add the mushrooms. Sauté for 2 or 3 minutes and add the garlic and thyme. Cook until the mushrooms give up all their liquid and then reabsorb it. Set aside.

3

In a saucepan over low heat, melt 3 tablespoons of butter and whisk in the flour. Stir over low heat until the roux is very lightly colored. Whisk in one cup of the turkey broth or chicken stock and bring to a simmer. Cook for 5 minutes, then add the cream and bring back to a simmer. Season with salt, cayenne, and lemon juice. Add the turkey, carrots, onions, and mushrooms to the sauce and stir. Let cool, then fold in the peas.

4

Preheat oven to 425°. Pour the mixture into a 1½-quart casserole. Roll out the pastry dough, to a size slightly larger than casserole and set atop turkey mixture. Double up the edges and press down with a fork to make a good seal. Cut a few slits in the dough to let steam escape and brush with an egg wash made from a beaten egg and a tablespoon of water. Place in oven. Bake 15 minutes. Lower the heat to 375° and bake until crust is nicely browned and puffed.

SPRING

Vermonters take spring quite seriously, possibly because it is the only season we have to ourselves. Fall brings leaf-peepers, winter brings skiers and snowmobilers, and summer brings bicyclists, hikers, and other generic vacationers. But almost no one comes to Vermont in spring, probably because it's hard to tell when it is here. One minute there's a promising, earthy whiff in the air, the next, a late storm has buried what's left of the woodpile under a foot of snow.

There is a surfeit of weather in Vermont during spring: snow, sleet, rain, and frost take their turn with sunny skies and soaring temperatures. And since weather is a major conversational staple here, spring fuels the conversational fires like no other season. The first harbinger of spring in Vermont is mud, mud so deep, so viscous, that it requires its own fifth season — "mud season" — during which dirt roads turn into a treacherous quicksand of brown muck that makes for trickier driving than the deepest snowfall. Several years ago, Virginia Garrison of Moretown got her car stuck in mud and was forced to abandon it overnight. It froze in place, and when the town grader pulled it out, the wires to the fuel pump were broken, the front wheels immobile, the brakes full of stones, and a joint in the front axle badly damaged. The grader ripped the bumper off. And the factory undercoating, Garrison said, was left in the mud "like a skeleton." Mud season strikes again.

I like mud season because it is the time of year when there is the least amount of work to do: the wood-burning furnace needs minimal stoking, there is little snow to shovel, there is no grass to mow, and the ground is too soggy

WHETHER IT'S GRILLED LEG OF LAMB, PASTA PRIMAVERA, OR CRACKED WHEAT SALAD — SHOWN HERE ON THE PORCH OF THE INN AT MONTPELIER, A POPULAR CAPITAL CITY HOSTELRY — THE FOODS OF SPRING ENHANCE VERMONT'S MOST ELUSIVE SEASON.

for gardening. There is little point in washing the car or cleaning the house. Exercise is easy to avoid: it's too muddy for jogging, there's not enough snow for skiing, snowmobiling, or snowshoeing, and it's far too cold to even think about a swim.

Gastronomically speaking, spring is full of pleasures, sneak previews, of the summer bounty to come. Fiddlehead ferns and marsh marigolds, dandelions, and innumerable wild edibles begin growing in fields, woods, and marshes, laying down the gauntlet to the adventurous cook sick of winter fare. Rhubarb — the springtime equivalent of zucchini (you can't give it away) except that it tastes and freezes better — appears in various incarnations at community suppers. Spring is trout season, and anyone who has tasted a fresh, pan-fried brookie knows the culinary pleasures of the stream.

The streams themselves, roiling with snow melt and rain, tear helter-skelter down the greening hillsides, demanding attention, announcing spring's arrival. The returning Canada geese announce it as well, honking out the news as they fly, in ragged V-formations, through skies made busy by wind-driven clouds of rain and snow. Spring is a time of discovery: the discovery of the garden hoe, the coffee mug, a tennis shoe, and other flotsam left outside the night before that first snowfall and never seen again until now. The discovery that the combination of washboard, frost heave, and pothole one navigates every morning on the way to work has separated the car from its muffler; and that the last snowplow of the season finally separated the mailbox from its pole. The discovery that both the roof and the basement still leak.

Spring is lambing time, a series of sleepless nights for the keepers of sheep, called on to midwife new lambs at all hours. In mid-May, peeping chicks arrive at the post office and hardware stores, and the part-time farmers among us, those who raise a few chickens for meat and eggs, can feel like real farmers for a while and talk knowledgeably about broiler mash and chicken lice. The first of three wild turkey seasons begins in May. Hunters say the keen-eyed, sharp-eared wild turkey, a bird native to Vermont, is firmer and leaner than domestic birds, and is one of the most challenging types of game to hunt.

But, most important for both the state's economy and psyche, spring is sugaring time. As Vermonters begin shaking off their cabin fever, the maple trees start sprouting buckets, and steam billows from the tin-roofed shacks that dot the countryside.

Tomato seedlings sprout on sunny windowsills. The first crop of parsley is harvested from the winterbox in the garden. Peepers carol in the marshes. Children vie for the honor of spying the first robin or the first crocus. The blood moves a bit quicker, the senses seem a bit keener. Despite the treachery of an April snowstorm, the perils of mud season, it becomes clear that winter has lost its grip.

We dare to say the words that were unthinkable in the frigid depths of January: summer is on its way. We know it's so because, after all, spring has finally arrived. Sort of.

Maple Sugaring

To truly appreciate sugaring, the process of turning maple sap into maple syrup, one must first appreciate mud season. Sap runs for a variety of botanical and hydraulic reasons having to do with all that thawing and freezing. Thus, many hundreds of Vermonters spend what the rest of the east coast calls spring slogging through the woods drilling holes into trees. As novelist Stephen Morris wrote in the *Sunday Rutland Herald*, "Mud season is so hellacious, it makes the boiling of tree sap seem like fun."

And sugaring *is* fun, if one is perversely Yankee enough to find fun in backbreaking and tedious labor that results in a splendid, luxurious, and ultimately practical product. For one thing, maple syrup is the first harvest of the year. For another, sugaring tends to be a convivial sort of activity, for there is nothing like a cloud of steam billowing out of the lopsided cupola atop a backyard sugarhouse to prompt friends and neighbors to drop by. And there are few more inviting places on a raw March day than a working sugarhouse, with its steamy, sweet warmth and the bustle of purposeful activity.

Sugaring season is the time of sugar-on-snow parties, featuring boiling syrup poured on snow; if the temperature of the syrup is right, it turns into crackly, sticky, delicious taffy when it hits the snow. Other sugaring staples are black coffee (milk for the kids), raised doughnuts, and sour pickles. I am fortunate enough to have neighbors who throw a big sugar-on-snow party every year, but there are also a number of commercial sugarhouses that offer such treats for a small fee.

Until recently, sugaring had remained virtually unchanged since practiced by the Abenakis: sap is collected and boiled over a fire until enough water evaporates and syrup remains. Now dramatic modernization has set in. Gone from many large sugaring operations are the galvanized steel buckets with their little peaked lids to keep the rain and most of the bugs out. Trees nowadays are often tapped using miles of plastic tubing. Some commercial sugarmakers speed the boiling process by investing in reverse osmosis machines, which force sap through tiny porous membranes to extract water. And some even use vacuum pumps; they are, a researcher told me, a little like milking machines for trees.

But it still takes about 40 gallons of maple sap to make a gallon of syrup. Sugarmakers, whether of the high- or low-tech variety, still tend to be some of the friendliest, hardest working people around. And the result is still the same: maple syrup in five grades (fancy, medium amber, dark amber, B, and C, the last sold for commercial use only). With roughly 500,000 gallons produced annually, Vermont leads the nation in maple syrup production and sugarmakers here aver with pride that Vermont syrup is unquestionably the best in the land.

Vermont cooks use maple syrup in pies and cookies, in glazing and stewing meat, in sweetening vinaigrettes and pots of baked beans, and in almost any way sugar can be used. Some people pour it over cold cereal. Others use it in tea and coffee. I prefer to save it for pancakes, waffles, and—when I can get it—Herb Odgen's stone-ground oatmeal. Others eat it plain, by the saucerful.

Whichever way one eats it, maple syrup is a spring surprise, a sweet secret hidden in the maples. It seems, in its way, like Nature's apology for the mud season. It's almost enough.

GRILLED MARINATED LEG OF LAMB

DELICIOUS FOR THE FIRST OUTDOOR MEAL OF THE YEAR.
SERVES 6 TO 8.

❧

*1 boneless leg of lamb (ask your butcher to bone your leg of lamb and
remove the fell—the membrane on the top side of the leg)
4 to 6 cloves garlic, 2 thinly sliced, 2 to 4 minced
2 tablespoons fresh rosemary or 1 tablespoon dried rosemary
1 tablespoon fresh thyme or 1½ teaspoons dried thyme
2 teaspoons black pepper, coarsely ground
1 tablespoon grated orange zest
½ cup olive oil*

1

Using a sharp knife, score the two large connected pieces of lamb with about 3 slashes 1 inch deep, or butterfly by splitting the leg down the center, cutting almost but not completely through, and open flat.

2

Using a sharp knife, make many slits into the fat side of the lamb and place garlic slices in each. In a nonaluminum dish combine rosemary, thyme, minced garlic, black pepper, zest, and olive oil. Place lamb in dish and turn several times to coat. Cover and refrigerate and allow to marinate for several hours or overnight.

3

Prepare a charcoal fire or gas grill. Remove lamb from marinade and place in a hinged rack over a lightly oiled grill. Cook one side until browned, turn and move further from the heat. Grill until browned but pink inside. Remove to a clean, warmed platter or plastic carving board and let rest, loosely covered, for 15 to 20 minutes. Serve thinly sliced with potato salad.

Asparagus and
Swiss Cheese Omelet

SIMPLE AND ATTRACTIVE. PERFECT FOR SUPPER OR BRUNCH.
SERVES 2.

8 asparagus spears, ends trimmed and peeled
5 eggs
1 tablespoon warm water
dash Tabasco
⅓ cup grated Swiss cheese
2 tablespoons unsalted butter
sour cream mixed with curry

1

Steam asparagus until crisp-tender and slice from the bottom into ¼-inch rounds, leaving 2-inch tips.

2

Beat eggs with 1 tablespoon of water and Tabasco.

3

In a large nonstick skillet over medium high heat, add butter and heat until it foams. Add asparagus rounds and cook until heated through. Add the egg mixture and cook until the edges stiffen slightly.

4

Remove from heat and lay asparagus tips lengthwise across the front third of the eggs perpendicular to the handle. Top with cheese and pass under broiler briefly to set the eggs.

5

Remove and slide the front third of the omelet up on the sloping side of the pan. Grasp the pan handle with your palm facing up, and set plate atop pan upside down, or slightly tilted. Invert pan so that plate is underneath, give the pan a little shake, and the omelet should fall neatly onto the plate. Season with salt, freshly ground pepper, and a dollop of curried sour cream.

STRAWBERRY AND BUTTERMILK SOUP

DELICIOUS AND REFRESHING. SERVES 4 TO 6.

4 egg yolks (optional: use pasteurized yolks if available)
1 tablespoon lemon juice
¼ cup granulated sugar
1 quart buttermilk
1 pint yogurt
2 pints strawberries, washed, hulled, and sliced
1 tablespoon honey
1 cup heavy cream, whipped (optional)
mint leaves

1

In a large mixing bowl, whisk egg yolks, lemon juice, and sugar together until fluffy and pale yellow. Set aside.

2

In a small mixing bowl, combine buttermilk and yogurt and fold into the yolk mixture.

3

Purée three quarters of the strawberries in a blender, food processor, or food mill (use a little of the soup base if necessary). Put the purée back in the buttermilk and yogurt base and stir in remaining berries. Adjust the sweet/tart balance with more lemon juice or honey. Chill soup and ladle into chilled bowls or cups and garnish with a dollop of unsweetened whipped cream and/or sprig of mint leaves.

CRACKED WHEAT SALAD WITH CHICKEN AND VEGETABLES

GREAT SHOWCASE FOR A SELDOM-USED GRAIN. TAKE OUT THE CHICKEN AND THIS SPICY TABOULI IS A VEGETARIAN TREAT.

—————————— ✵ ——————————

4 boneless skinless chicken breasts, trimmed (1 pound total)
1 clove garlic, peeled and smashed
1 tablespoon parsley, chopped
juice of 1 lemon
olive oil to coat
1 teaspoon salt
1 cup bulgur (cracked wheat)
4 scallions, sliced
1½ cups sugar snap peas or snow peas, trimmed, blanched, and cut into ½-inch lengths
1 small zucchini, washed and finely diced
1 tomato, seeded and diced
1 red pepper, seeded and diced
½ cup parsley, chopped
½ cup romaine lettuce, chopped
1 tablespoon white wine vinegar
1 small hot chili, seeded and diced (optional)
½ cup olive oil
large leaves romaine lettuce
pita bread, lightly toasted and cut in wedges
¼ cup crumbled feta cheese
1 or 2 tomatoes, cut in wedges
olives

1

Rinse chicken breasts and pat dry. Place them in a shallow dish. In a small bowl, combine garlic, parsley, juice of ½ lemon, salt, freshly ground pepper, and oil. Pour over chicken, turn to coat, cover, and marinate for several hours in the refrigerator.

2

Cook chicken under preheated broiler or on a lightly oiled grill for about 3 to 4 minutes per side, or until no longer pink inside. Set aside for 10 minutes, then shred into small pieces with your fingers.

3

Bring 1½ cups of salted water to a boil and pour over bulgur. Let sit 45 minutes and drain. Combine bulgur with vegetables, parsley, and chopped romaine.

4

Prepare vinaigrette by combining vinegar, 1 tablespoon of lemon juice, chili, salt, and pepper. Whisk in ½ cup of olive oil. Moisten vegetable and bulgur mixture with vinaigrette and place on romaine lined plates. Arrange shredded chicken on top and garnish with pita triangles, feta cheese, tomatoes, and olives.

THIS CRACKED WHEAT
SALAD WITH CHICKEN AND
VEGETABLES COULD BE A
LIGHT LUNCH OR MIGHT
AUGMENT A LARGER MEAL.
RECIPE ON PREVIOUS
PAGE.

Beef and Vegetable Stir Fry

How to make a one-pound steak satisfy
four big appetites. Serves 4.

— ❧ —

1 pound strip or top sirloin steak
2 tablespoons peanut oil
2 tablespoons soy sauce
2 tablespoons white vinegar
1 dried hot chili, seeds removed and crushed or ½ teaspoon cayenne
¾ cup pineapple juice
1 tablespoon cornstarch
1 tablespoon garlic, minced
1 tablespoon ginger, minced
1 small red pepper, diced
1 red onion, thinly sliced
6 radishes, trimmed and thickly sliced
6 ounces small mushrooms, quartered
6 ounces sugar snap or snow peas, trimmed, cut into ¾-inch lengths
3 scallions, cut into 1-inch lengths
1 cup mung bean sprouts

1

Trim the steak of all fat and cut into ½-inch cubes. In a bowl, whisk together soy, vinegar, chili, cayenne, pineapple juice, and cornstarch.

2

Heat a wok or large skillet with sloped sides until hot. Add 1 tablespoon of peanut oil and swirl to coat pan. Add beef and let brown well on one side. Turn and let brown on the other side. Cook, tossing occasionally until rare. Strain and set aside. Wipe out wok, reheat, and add remaining peanut oil. Add garlic and ginger and cook until fragrant. Add pepper and onion and cook until color is heightened. Add radishes and mushrooms and cook a few more minutes. Add peas, cooked beef, and pineapple juice mixture. Bring to the edge of a boil until liquid clears and thickens. Add scallions and bean sprouts. Remove from heat. Serve over brown rice.

CREAM OF ASPARAGUS SOUP

IT'S HARD TO SACRIFICE FRESH ASPARAGUS IN THE SPRING,
BUT THIS IS A WORTHY WAY TO DO IT.

———————————— ❧ ————————————

1 pound asparagus, woody ends removed and bottoms peeled
handful spinach leaves, stems removed, and washed
¼ cup unsalted butter
1 medium onion, finely diced
2 scallions, top and bottom sliced
2 quarts chicken stock
1 medium baking potato, peeled and thinly sliced
½ pound sugar snap peas, trimmed, washed, and cut into ½-inch lengths or
fresh shelled peas
1 cup heavy cream
salt
freshly ground white pepper
pinch freshly grated nutmeg
2 tablespoons grated Romano cheese

1

Cut asparagus from the bottom into ¼-inch rounds, leaving 1½-inch
tips. Steam tips until bright green and tender. Chill and set aside.

2

In a small pot over medium heat, cook spinach, covered, in the water
that stays with it after washing, just until wilted. Chill and set aside.

3

In a large nonstick skillet, melt butter, add onions and scallions, and
cook until soft. Add asparagus rounds and cook 3 to 4 minutes, stirring occasionally.

4

Add potatoes and stock and bring to a simmer. Cook until potatoes
are just tender. Add peas and cook for 1 minute more. Meanwhile,
gently heat cream in a small saucepan.

5

In a blender combine spinach and most of the asparagus tips. Save a few asparagus tips for garnish. Add enough soup base to cover the vegetables. Purée to a smooth, bright green. Carefully add more soup base and repeat if necessary.

6

In a large pot combine purée and heavy cream and bring to the edge of a simmer. Season with salt and a small amount of pepper and nutmeg. Ladle into hot cups or bowls. Garnish with asparagus tips cut in half lengthwise and a pinch of Romano cheese.

FIDDLEHEADS WITH
BROWN BUTTER AND CRUMBS

A GREAT WAY TO ENJOY FIDDLEHEADS
WITHOUT THE BITTER AFTERTASTE. SERVES 4.

1 pound fresh fiddleheads
1 hard-cooked egg, peeled and chopped
2 tablespoons parsley, chopped
½ teaspoon grated orange zest
1 tablespoon fresh orange juice
1 tablespoon fresh lemon juice
6 tablespoons unsalted butter
1 clove garlic, minced
4 tablespoons fresh bread crumbs

1

Rub fuzz or brownish covering off fiddleheads and wash in cold water.

2

Steam until bright green and tender-crisp. Drain well and arrange on a serving platter. Sprinkle with egg, parsley, zest, and orange and lemon juice.

3

In a small skillet heat butter and garlic until butter foams. Add bread crumbs and cook until they are lightly browned. Arrange over fiddleheads and serve.

Vegetarian Linguine Primavera

For lovers of goat cheese. Serves 3 to 4.

---

1 pound linguine
¼ cup unsalted butter
2 tablespoons virgin olive oil
2 shallots, minced
1 cup morels or button mushrooms, sliced
½ cup fresh Vermont goat cheese, crumbled
1 cup fiddleheads, brownish covering rubbed off, washed
1 cup Swiss chard, washed and tightly packed
½ cup radishes, trimmed and sliced thinly
pinch fresh thyme or salt
½ cup mozzarella (¼-inch cubes)
4 tablespoons chives, chopped
⅓ cup toasted pine nuts

1

Cook linguine al dente in 1 gallon boiling salted water, lightly oiled. Drain and cool. Meanwhile, steam fiddleheads until crisp-tender, reserving liquid. Steam chard until wilted, drain and chop.

2

In a large nonstick skillet over medium heat, heat butter and olive oil. Add the mushrooms and shallots. Cook until shallots are softened and mushrooms give up their liquid. Add thyme and reserved fiddlehead liquid; simmer. Whisk in goat cheese. Add fiddleheads, chard, and radishes. Taste and adjust seasonings.

3

Reheat the pasta and drain. Add to the sauce, adjusting the consistency with a couple of tablespoons of the pasta cooking water if necessary. Remove from heat, add the cubed mozzarella, and toss gently. Transfer to heated platters and garnish with chives, pine nuts, and freshly ground pepper.

STRAWBERRY RHUBARB COBBLER

A NICE CHANGE OF PACE FROM STRAWBERRY RHUBARB PIE.
THIS DISH LOOKS QUITE ELEGANT SERVED IN PARFAIT GLASSES.
SERVES 4.

3 cups rhubarb, cut into ½-inch lengths
2 cups strawberries, quartered
¾ to 1 cup sugar, depending on ripeness of berries
6 tablespoons flour
pinch salt
pinch grated lemon zest
¼ cup rolled oats
¼ cup flour
¼ cup brown sugar
4 tablespoons butter
¼ cup lightly toasted pecans, chopped
pinch cinnamon

1

Preheat oven to 375°. Rub 8-inch-square baking pan with butter.

2

In a large mixing bowl, combine rhubarb, berries, sugar, flour, salt, and zest. Mix well and turn into baking pan.

3

In a large mixing bowl, combine oats, flour, brown sugar, pecans, and cinnamon and spread over fruit mixture. Bake for 30 minutes or until filling is set and topping is browned. Let cool until warm. Top with whipped cream or ice cream.

STRAWBERRY RHUBARB
COBBLER, SERVED WITH
A TOUCH OF ELEGANCE IN
PARFAIT GLASSES,
EMBODIES THE TASTE OF
SPRINGTIME.

SAUTÉED BROOK TROUT
(RAINBOW OR BROWN)

THIS SIMPLE RECIPE LETS THE TASTE OF THE FRESH TROUT
SHINE THROUGH. SERVES 4.

¼ cup flour
¼ cup corn flour or very fine cornmeal
pinch garlic powder
¼ teaspoon salt
freshly ground black pepper
four 10-inch brook trout or eight 6-inch brook trout
1 cup milk
dash Tabasco
¼ cup peanut oil
1 tablespoon unsalted butter
lemon wedges for garnish

1

In a long, shallow dish, combine flour, corn flour, garlic powder, salt, and pepper. Set aside.

2

Clean the trout. In a small bowl, combine milk, Tabasco, and pour over trout. Remove the trout from the milk and roll to coat evenly in the flour mixture. Place on a dry plate.

3

In a heavy cast-iron skillet over medium heat, heat oil. Add butter and when it foams add the trout. Cook to brown on one side and turn. Cook for a little less than 10 minutes per inch of thickness at the thickest part of the fish. Remove from skillet carefully onto paper to drain. Place on heated plates. Serve with lemon wedges or moistened with browned butter mixed with lemon juice and parsley.

SAUTÉED MORELS WITH FRESH HERBS

NOW THAT YOU FINALLY FOUND THEM,
HERE'S A WAY TO COOK THEM. SERVES 4.

½ pound morels (morchella esculenta)
4 tablespoons unsalted butter
1 large shallot, finely minced, or 2 scallion whites
1 tablespoon finely diced red pepper
1 tablespoon finely diced green pepper
¼ teaspoon fresh thyme
1 tablespoon parsley, chopped
1 tablespoon chives, chopped
salt
mushroom soy sauce (use regular soy sauce as a substitute if necessary)
4 slices firm country style bread, toasted and lightly buttered
2 tablespoons heavy cream (optional)

1

Brush any dirt from morels, trim if necessary. Depending on their size, leave morels whole, or cut in ½-inch or ¼-inch slices.

2

In a medium nonstick skillet, heat butter to foaming and add shallots and peppers. Cook just until the color of the peppers is brightened. Add morels, stirring well to coat with butter. Cook gently until the morels give up all their liquid and then start to reabsorb it. Add thyme and parsley and simmer another minute. (At this stage a few ounces of cream or a couple of tablespoons of butter could be added. If using cream, simmer to reduce it slightly.) Season with salt and soy and spoon over toast. Garnish with chopped chives.

SHREDDED DUCK AND NOODLE SALAD

EXCELLENT WITH CHICKEN BUT WORTH FINDING
THE DUCK IF YOU CAN. SERVES 4.

❧

4 duck legs (if duck is unavailable, substitute chicken legs)
1 small ginger root, peeled and minced
2 cloves garlic, peeled, minced
pinch chili flakes
2 cups chicken stock
2 carrots, peeled
2 cucumbers, peeled
2 zucchini (skinned)
1 pound linguine or cappellini, cooked al dente
¼ cup rice wine vinegar
¼ cup soy sauce
¼ cup duck braising liquid
2 tablespoons maple syrup
3 cloves garlic, peeled and smashed
1 thumb-sized piece of ginger, peeled, sliced, smashed, minced
1 or 2 dried hot chilies (dry toasted in teflon pan, seeds removed)
2 tablespoons cilantro, chopped
2 tablespoons sesame seeds, toasted
1 tablespoon sesame oil

1

In a heavy-bottomed skillet over low heat, place duck legs skin side down and cook until lightly browned. Pour off all but 1 tablespoon of fat and add garlic and ginger. Stir, cooking until fragrant. Turn duck legs skin side up. Add chili flakes and chicken stock and bring to a boil. Bring to a simmer and cook, covered, until legs are tender, about 1 hour. Remove skin and shred meat with your fingers. Reserve a small amount of cooking broth.

2

Cut carrot, cucumber, and zucchini into the longest, thinnest slices possible. Use all the carrot, the cucumber just until you reach the seeds, and zucchini skin only ⅛ inch deep. Blanch or steam the carrot for 1 minute in boiling water.

3

Prepare vinaigrette by combining rice wine vinegar, soy, duck broth from step 1, maple syrup, garlic, ginger, and chilies in a small pot over low heat. Bring to a simmer, strain, and reserve.

4

Combine noodles, half the duck, and the vegetables in a large bowl. Toss well. Add the vinaigrette and mix. Transfer to serving plates. Arrange remaining duck over the noodles and sprinkle with sesame oil, cilantro, and toasted sesame seeds.

PAN-FRIED CATFISH (BULLHEADS)

THERE ARE SEVERAL VARIETIES OF CATFISH.
ANY OF THEM WILL DO FOR THIS RECIPE SINCE ALL CATFISH
HAVE THE FIRM WHITE FLESH CHARACTERISTIC OF THE SPECIES.
SERVES 4.

½ cup peanut or vegetable oil
1 tablespoon butter
4 dressed bullheads, gutted with head, tail, and skin removed or
four 6- to 8-ounce catfish or other white fish fillets
(catfish fillets are firmer than most and therefore preferable)
salt
cayenne
freshly ground black pepper
½ cup flour
2 tablespoons olive oil
1 clove garlic, minced
½ small onion, finely diced
½ cup fish stock
¼ cup clam juice plus ¼ cup water
2 tomatoes, peeled and seeded
2 scallions, diced
2 tablespoons unsalted butter
lime wedges for garnish

1

In a pie tin, combine flour, salt, cayenne, and black pepper. Roll the bullheads or filets in the mixture and set aside.

2

In a heavy skillet over medium high heat, heat oil. Add butter and place filets in skillet. Cook until brown on one side. Turn and cook until the fish just starts to flake (catfish flesh is denser than most fish and cooks somewhat slowly).

Remove fish to drain on paper towels. Pour off all the fat in the skillet and add the olive oil. Heat and add the garlic and onion. Cook until softened. Add the fish stock or clam juice and water. Add the tomatoes and simmer until the liquid has reduced by half. Add the scallions and whisk in the butter. Adjust the seasonings. Place fish on warmed plates and pour sauce over each. Serve with lime wedges and coleslaw.

POTATO LEEK SOUP WITH SPRING GREENS

COMFORT FOOD FOR A SPRING DAY. SERVES 4 TO 6.

2 tablespoons unsalted butter
¼ cup unsalted butter, diced
1 small onion, finely diced
3 or 4 white or light green leeks, cleaned, sliced, rinsed and dried
2 or 3 medium baking potatoes, peeled, finely diced, and placed in
2-quarts cold water
2 cups spinach or wild leek greens or watercress
or a combination, thinly sliced
2 tablespoons chives, chopped

In a heavy-bottomed saucepan over medium low heat, heat butter until it foams. Add the onion and leeks and cook until slightly softened. Add potatoes and water and bring to a simmer. Season with salt and cook until potatoes are tender. Stir in greens, adjust the seasoning and pour immediately into warmed soup cups or bowls. Garnish with butter cubes and chopped chives.

THE ADDITION OF
SPINACH OR WATERCRESS
ADDS SAVOR TO THIS
SATISFYING YET LIGHT
POTATO LEEK SOUP.
RECIPE ON PREVIOUS
PAGE.

Chopped Lamb Steak with Chutney Butter

Serves 4.

✿

1½ pounds ground lamb
1 tablespoon unsalted butter
2 teaspoons curry powder
1 medium onion, diced
4 cloves garlic, minced
2 teaspoons cumin
1 teaspoon coriander
½ cup parsley, chopped
4 tablespoons cilantro, chopped
salt and cayenne pepper to taste
½ cup unsalted butter, softened
4 tablespoons mango chutney, chopped
2 tablespoons mint leaves, chopped

1

Heat butter in a nonstick skillet over medium heat, add onion and cook until transparent. Add garlic and curry powder. Cook, stirring gently, until garlic is softened. Cool.

2

In a large bowl, combine lamb, onion mix, and remaining ingredients. Work with hands until the lamb feels a little sticky then divide into 4 equal portions. Shape into ovals ¾ inch thick. Set aside.

3

Prepare chutney butter by beating together butter, chutney, and mint in a small bowl until smooth. Shape the mixture into a roll and wrap in parchment paper or plastic wrap. Chill until stiff.

4

Broil or grill steaks until browned but pink inside. Top with a slice of chutney butter and garnish with lemon wedges.

GRILLED SALMON WITH
MONTPELLIER BUTTER

A LONGTIME FAVORITE AT MONTPELIER'S ELM STREET CAFÉ.
SERVES 4.

—————————— ❧ ——————————

1 handful spinach leaves, trimmed
1 bunch watercress
¼ cup parsley
¼ cup chives, cut
2 tablespoons fresh tarragon or chervil or 1 tablespoon dried tarragon
4 scallion whites, minced
2 small sour gherkins, chopped
2 anchovy fillets, minced
1 clove garlic, minced
1 tablespoon capers, rinsed, drained, and minced
dash tarragon vinegar
3 hard-cooked egg yolks
1 uncooked egg yolk
½ cup unsalted butter, softened
¼ cup olive oil
salt
freshly ground black pepper
cayenne
1½ pounds salmon fillet, skinned and cut into 4 portions
peanut oil

—————————————————————————————

1

In a 6-quart pot, boil 4 quarts of water. Place spinach, watercress, and herbs in a strainer and immerse in water for 15 seconds. Remove and run under cold water. Drain and pat very dry. Chop finely.

2

To prepare Montpellier butter: In a small bowl, combine herb mixture with the minced scallions, gherkins, capers, and garlic. Mince anchovies and garlic together into a paste and add to mixture. Add the egg yolk, vinegar, and softened butter and whisk until smooth. Drizzle the olive oil into the mixture. (This can also be done in a food processor.) Push the butter through a fine strainer, if desired, and season to taste. At room temperature the consistency should be similar to a very thick pancake batter.

3

Lightly oil a charcoal grill rack. Season salmon with salt, pepper, and cayenne and lightly coat with peanut oil. Put fillets on the grill, skin side up. Cook until marked and turn. Cook 2 to 3 minutes longer. The salmon should start to flake when probed and be very moist. Place on warm plates and add a pat of Montpellier butter to each portion. Serve with boiled new potatoes, sugar snap peas, and sautéed tomatoes.

ROAST CHICKEN WITH
GARLIC AND HERBS

DRESSES UP A SUNDAY DINNER. SERVES 2 TO 4.

3½-pound whole frying chicken
2 tablespoons unsalted butter, softened
2 cloves garlic, minced
1 head of garlic, split
1 tablespoon, chives, chopped
1 tablespoon parsley, chopped
1 sprig fresh rosemary
3 or 4 sprigs fresh thyme
2 teaspoons butter
3 cups chicken stock
1 tablespoon arrowroot

1

Place baking pan and wire rack in oven and preheat to 400°. Remove livers, gizzards, hearts, and necks from chicken cavity. Rinse chicken with cold water, inside and out, and pat dry.

2

To prepare the herb butter, combine butter, garlic, chives, and parsley and blend well, seasoning to taste. Loosen skin covering the breast of the chicken from the neck end and spread flesh liberally with herb butter. Bruise the rosemary sprig with the side of a knife and rub over the chicken. Place the rosemary, thyme sprigs, and garlic head in the cavity. Season inside and out with salt and freshly ground pepper.

3

Truss the chicken using soft twine. Rub remaining butter on outside of chicken and place on preheated wire rack in baking pan. Place in top ½ of oven and roast for 30 minutes. Baste with pan juices, reduce oven temperature to 350°, and roast for an additional 30 to 40 minutes, or until juices run clear when thigh is pierced with a skewer. Remove to a warm spot and let sit at least 20 minutes.

4

Remove fat from the bake pan and add a small amount of chicken stock. Place the bake pan on a low burner and cook, scraping up any coagulated juices. Add the rest of the chicken stock and some of the thyme or garlic from the chicken cavity and simmer until reduced by half. Dissolve 1 tablespoon of arrowroot in 2 tablespoons of cold water and add to the simmering stock. Bring to a boil and cook for 30 seconds. Strain. Adjust seasonings to taste.

5

Disjoint and carve chicken, arrange on warm dinner plates, and serve with sauce. Accompany with potatoes and green vegetables.

MAPLE-GLAZED CORNED BEEF

SERVES 6 TO 8.

4 pounds corned brisket, rinsed
2 onions, sliced
2 carrots, sliced
6 tablespoons maple syrup
2 tablespoons brown sugar
4 tablespoons whole grain mustard
2 tablespoons cider vinegar
pinch allspice

1

In a large pot place corned beef, onions, and carrots and cover with cold water. Bring to a simmer and cook gently for 3 to 4 hours, or until tender. Remove and pat dry.

2

In a small bowl, combine syrup, brown sugar, mustard, vinegar, and allspice to make a paste. Preheat oven to 375°. Spread paste evenly over corned beef and place in oven for 10 to 15 minutes until paste glazes.

INDEX

✿

Marialisa Calta is a nationally known food writer whose work appears regularly in *Eating Well* magazine and the *New York Times*. Her syndicated column appears in newspapers around the country. She is a graduate of the Columbia School of Journalism and a former reporter for the *Barre-Montpelier Times Argus* and the *Providence Journal*. She lives in Calais with her two daughters and her husband, who is also a journalist.